Global Banking Strategy

To Roseline, Guy-René, and Christophe

Global Banking Strategy

Financial Markets and Industrial Decay

Hervé de Carmoy

Basil Blackwell

First published in France as *Stratégie bancaire: le refus de la dérive*,

First published 1990

Basil Blackwell, Inc.
3 Cambridge Center
Cambridge, Massachusetts 02142, USA

Basil Blackwell Ltd
108 Cowley Road, Oxford, OX4 1JF, UK

British Library Cataloguing in Publication Data

A CIP catalogue record for this book is available from the British Library

Library of Congress Cataloging in Publication Data

Carmoy, Hervé de.
[Stratégie bancaire. English]
Global Banking Strategy: financial markets and industrial decay / Hervé de Carmoy.
p. cm.
Translation of: Stratégie bancaire.
ISBN 1-55786-245-1 (hard)
1. Banks and banking. 2. Banks and banking–Europe.
3. Banks and banking–United States. 4. Banks and banking–Japan.
5. Strategic planning. 6. Competition, International. I. Title.
HG1573.C3713 1990 332-dc20 90-1163 CIP

Typeset in 11 on 13pt Bembo
by Hope Services (Abingdon) Ltd
Printed in Great Britain by
T. J. Press, Padstow, Cornwall

Contents

◆

Preface

GLOBAL BANKING STRATEGY was born of a dialogue which began nearly twenty years ago with Professor Alain Cotta on the nature and scope of transformations that were underway in the world banking industry. These exchanges of view had the merit of demonstrating that academic and practitioner could talk to one another and even agree. This book would have never come about had it not been for the encouragement of Alain Cotta and the diligence with which he followed its writing.

Five years as Director and Chief Executive, Global Banking, of the Midland Bank Group in London and Chairman of the Thomas Cook Group helped me in the search for documentation, in the choice of examples, and, of course, in the development of a practical approach.

Finally, I would like to thank Sir Kit McMahon and the Midland Bank board for their trust, and John Brooks and the Midland Group staff for their loyalty and commitment.

H. de C.

◇

Introduction

◆

During the decades of exceptional growth after World War II there was a lively debate on industrial strategy. What should we produce? How should we produce it? Where should we expand? These were the questions senior management in industry was continually asking itself. Banks, on the other hand, sailed on in comfortable tranquility. Their activities, dominated by a form of intermediation which dated back a century and a half – short-term borrowing from private individuals to finance long-term lending to the state or industry – were not changed in any significant way. And this status quo was reinforced by a *de facto* protectionism which ensured each star in the banking constellation its own semi-private preserve. This situation fostered a kind of caste system, in that each member of the banking community had the impression that it held an allotted role in a ritual instituted long ago. Until the last two decades, then, banks, though haunted by an obsessive fear of industrial risk, felt that they performed both a more hidden and a more distinguished function in the social and economic order.

FOUR FACTORS OF CHANGE

Now, nearly twenty years after the major outbreak of monetary turbulence that marked the beginning of the 1970s, that situation has changed. And like a block of marble from which the chisel has only half freed the statue, it is beginning to reveal the future form of banking.

A review of four major factors, which constitute the theme of the first part of this book, shows the time scale of these emerging changes.

The first is the change of banks' production methods due to the extremely rapid application of technology to most areas of finance. Of all the reasons for the transformation of the banking universe, this factor looms largest, carrying with it the most far-reaching changes and affecting the entire provision of banking services.

In the early 1970s, the world of the quill pen, though still a familiar one in Saudi Arabia, had already given way in the developed world to that of the computer: but the worldwide spread of information, which was to shake the entire banking business, had not yet permeated the banks. Yesterday, lightly equipped, they ensured the financing of massive industrial investment; tomorrow they will have at their disposal powerful tools: satellites and virtually instantaneous communication. They will also have to invest in financing both the most strategic and the most costly projects of world economic development. Banks with the ability and the means to adapt will be tomorrow's winners.

The second factor concerns competition. Developments in technology are critical, but they will not alone shape the destiny of banks for the rest of the century. Even before its spectacular intensification, technology had transformed the traditional domain of banking by adding the private individuals' banking business to the great historical market of intermediation and by modifying the traditional relations of banks with sovereign borrowers. No longer was there a single banking service, but in its place a vastly extended range of activities, each of which formed a market subject to the workings of free competition. The nature and intensity of competition has become at least as important a factor as technical progress is in shaping the sovereign loan business, the corporate banking market, the private individual banking business and the securities and money market businesses. Moreover, competition and technology are linked because it is virtually impossible to compete effectively in any of the sectors mentioned above without access to sophisticated technology.

Today, the continual drive to adapt and to compete is facilitated in some cases and impeded in others by the state and its regulatory authorities. Deregulation, the third of our four factors, embodies the end of an age when banks were kept under close surveillance by the public authorities, purely because they managed and had the power to create currency. This historical situation explains the distinctions between several types of banks as well as the separation of banks and financial institutions. Specialized banks were that much more protected: in the United States, for example, each state had its own commercial banks and each European state, perhaps, had three or four domestic banks with nationwide activities, which constituted stable oligopolies; and Japan's newly founded banks were shielded from competition by the most meticulous centralism in Asia.

Deregulation has a lot more to do with technological advances than with ideology. The launching of world telecommunications satellites and the setting-up of vast value-added networks do not mesh easily with all the preserves and controls of which the bank was still both beneficiary and victim twenty years ago. Nevertheless, the retreat of public protection has not simply increased banks' strategic freedom. Certainly, new products can be created today which could not yesterday. Certainly, the banks now have access to markets from which they had been excluded. Certainly, they can consider and contract alliances which yesterday would have been inconceivable. But there are two sides to this coin, and on the other are the additional responsibilities they have acquired – which in time generate their own regulations – and new controls, on a global dimension, arising from the new risks of internationalization.

The fourth factor lies in the serious problem of human adaptation to the acceleration of technical, commercial, and regulatory changes. Techniques may change but people remain much more bound to their origins, their training and their history. Technical changes might be introduced fairly easily, with firms adapting gradually to cope with technical progress but no organization, however well managed, would be able to reorientate human behavior and mentalities so quickly, or so smoothly. How are mature bankers to be encouraged to use the new techniques deployed on capital markets or borrowed from industrial marketing? The recent history of the money markets shows that implementing those changes called for the contribution of people from another generation capable of assimilating and practicing additional trades.

Barriers of age, training, method of activity, and remuneration can weaken capacity to act and to seize opportunities. Human resource management has therefore become at least as crucial as that of technology. The two are in fact intimately linked. The efficiency of tomorrow's bank will depend on its capacity to mobilize and to unite the complex groups of people required by the development of technical, commercial and institutional constraints. These people must therefore be given a plan: that is, a strategy.

STRATEGY FOR COMPETITION AND CONCENTRATION

The end point of this strategy is clear, at least in the medium and long term. All banks must achieve the strongest possible growth in profits and net assets. Over a ten-year period, growth in earnings and growth in total assets should, for global banks, coincide. Faster growth in assets than in earnings may be a symptom of overtrading on equity, poor cost control, and/or a deterioration in the quality of the assets; conversely, faster growth in earnings than in assets should raise a question mark over how much the bank is investing for the future in terms of human resources, information technology, or low-yielding assets serving as seedcorn for long-term beneficial relationships.

Strategic reorientation is clearly not achieved by addressing only the technical, commercial, regulatory, and human constraints: one must also consider changes in the banking sector as a whole. This is a clear and pressing requirement for all banks today, and an examination of the recent evolution of the world's banks is the subject of part II of this book.

It is not purely documentary. The rapid change in the banking hierarchy during these last few years thwarts any attempt to analyze the almost immediate consequences of a bank's strategy from the outside.

One need only think back: ten years ago, the Bank of America was the second largest bank in the world; it declined dramatically in less than two years, overwhelmed by the agricultural and industrial collapse of a region of the United States which only recently was still considered invulnerable: California. Ten years ago, Japanese banking, highly protected and controlled and in generally only moderately successful, contented itself with managing one of the most important savings industries in the world. For a long time it remained insular. Today, nine – tomorrow, perhaps ten – Japanese banks are among the ten largest in the world; and Citicorp, the standard-bearer of American banks, now represents no more than a decreasing percentage, in terms of assets, of the Dai Ichi Kangyo Bank, emblem of Japanese financial power. Japanese banks have gone international, forced to recognize the global influence of their currency and their industry. They play a key role in Japan's strategy of conquest, which by the end of the century will have become as apparent as the spectacular and lasting advance of their industry.

The increased concentration of banking fundamentally changes the conditions of the world game. Up until 1973, the large number of banks with a world strategy – say the 150–200 largest concerns – ensured the existence of real competition. Now everything seems to indicate that fewer banks means less – and different – competition. We are probably at the beginning of a long period which will see the gradual formation of a world banking oligopoly. The strategic questions faced by all the players in this new phase are twofold: to be or not to be a part of this world oligopoly in the more or less faraway future; and, as part of it, how to survive and in what form?

The last chapter of this book is devoted to these two questions. To limit ourselves to banks which can at present claim to be world-scale, it focuses on three major responses: the strategy of conquest, the response of all those who believe they are the best placed in this race toward concentration; the strategy of change, the response of all those who realize that maintenance of the status quo would condemn them to exclusion from this oligopoly and therefore to a subordinate role, in fact as subcontractors; and the strategy of consolidation, the response of all those who think that time will be on their side if they persevere in their determination.

PART I

THE CONSTRAINTS

I

◇

The Technological Constraint

◆

TECHNOLOGICAL PROGRESS: THE BACKGROUND

Technology has an ambivalent significance for managers. On the one hand, it is an operative tool which affects the efficiency of action; on the other, it poses a constraint that can be overcome only by means of appropriate changes in strategy. Moreover, technology gives banks the ability to create and distribute new financial products both for the corporate as well as the private individual market. Success and competition in these fields generate demand which, in turn, generates its own additional constraints on the banks.

The general characteristics of technological progress

The changes in the firm's structures imposed by technology move the frontiers of its activity and at the same time affect its competitive position. Accordingly technology is an essential element of corporate strategy – not only because of its implications for the firm's own production activity, but also because of its potential use by competitors. What, then, are the effects of technological innovation on a bank's products and services? What factors govern its adoption by a bank and its competitors?

Technology and strategic choices[1]

Technology affects the growth of banks' corporate activities in both the differentiation of products and sector diversification, two elements that provide both comparative advantages and new strategic constraints.

Differentiation enables a bank to respond to strategic constraints over time by being able to offer a range of products which lends the bank earnings stability. A one-product firm which adopts a simplified strategy limited to that single product is still dependent for its entire earnings on the one product – even though its chances of success are a matter of probability. Technology is capable of helping banks overcome product obsolescence as well as generate new products which diversify the earnings base.

But it is diversification – moving from one sector of activity to another – more than differentiation, which matters in the life of financial institutions. No firm's activity can be described solely in terms of differentiation: all have a range of products which place them in different sectors. As a result, firms have been able to offer products which were traditionally offered by firms in other sectors. This has been particularly the case with banks, insurance companies, and stockbrokers. The entry into banking on the London market of the Japanese broker Daiwa is a striking but typical example.

Technological innovation, spawning products that are not so much diversified as completely different, offers an escape from sectoral obsolescence by adopting new sectors and abandoning old ones. It allows banks to diversify their markets and, if their competitive activities are well chosen, to achieve stable profits. Finally, technology is conducive to decentralizing management since diversification fosters modular management structures with a sharper focus on individuals' responsibilities and a close relationship with the market.

These are great advantages; yet the introduction of new technologies also induces new constraints capable of generating real difficulties.

The first crucial thing to realize is that there is no longer a common body of technology in banking. The explosion of information technology has resulted in increasing differentiation of systems, approaches, and hardware. Maintaining a high level of technological performance simultaneously on several markets therefore requires good organization, tight cost control, and a wise choice of investment levels. It also requires careful selection of the systems to ensure compatibility.

Secondly, technological innovation may enable firms to come up with new products, but it cannot guarantee that they will *sell*. This difficulty looms larger in sectors that have reached maturity, and especially in banking, which came very late to appreciation of the importance of marketing.[2]

Finally, the generation of products or sectors by new technology creates additional costs which will increase with the degree of diversification.

The difficulties posed by the introduction of new technology are therefore added to the actual costs of any innovation (cost of design, research, development, etc.). The choice of a new technology, of course, must take into account not only that data, but also the fact that, by acting on production costs, the newly introduced technology ensures the entrepreneur a profit margin above that of his competitors. The evolution of such a margin in time depends on several factors, including the nature of the new technology.

Different technologies

A useful distinction can be drawn between the nature and effects of simpler and more complex technologies. Simple technology does not call into question the bank's production process, the relationships between the different factors of production, or the nature of the product it deals with. Its sole function is probably to reduce on overhead or modify a product's traditional features. The more complex technologies might radically change the structure of the workforce and management, and have far-reaching implications for costs and employment levels.

These two forms of technology have different modes of

application; the first type is immediately applicable in the company, whereas the introduction of the second depends on several factors, including the behavior of other firms, the degree of resistance among the work-force, and, more decisively, the ability of the managerial staff to induce the necessary process of change. Finally, there is an opportunity cost involved in the simple fact that any entrepreneur who substitutes a new technology for an old one depreciates the previously existing capital which still had production capability.

In banking, the effects of a particular technology on the company's structures are less important than the competitive advantages which it procures.

Banking confronts the technological revolution

The developments in banking have led banks toward the provision of services based on telecommunications technology, while office technology has grown in importance and is now vital for internal bank management. Office technology offers both an information service and a communications service to management. Its future must see improved circulation of information among different hardware and the further development of local area networks and so-called complete networks. The expansion of this segment reflects the pressure to establish high-quality, large-flow digital networks.

Developments in telecommunications reflect the demand for services offering high-flow networks, characterized by the convergence of the integrated services digital network (ISDN) and bank-wide networks.

Financing the development of these networks on a world scale is an activity at present only within the reach of a small number of large and financially powerful but, especially, world-oriented organizations. Financial power is only one of the criteria. The most important distinction here seems to be that between banks of a global character and the others, which will become specialized according to geography, sector (e.g. J.P. Morgan: money-market activities, large corporate accounts, cash management), or products (e.g. Cetelem).

For a bank to be truly global it must fulfil several conditions:

- it must have its head office in one of the six major world financial markets;
- it must have a solid, direct presence in Europe, the United States, and Asia;
- it must have a significant market share of large corporate accounts, personal banking, medium-sized companies, and sovereign borrowers;
- it must offer the array of products required by these different market segments.

This type of institution needs to address the possibilities offered by the communications satellite. Global banks will tend to monopolize a growing share of activities in the markets where they operate. They will be led to play the role of world counterparts. Considering the sums at stake ($3 trn–$4 trn a day), this requires sizeable investment. These operations – hitherto recorded off balance sheet which are in the process of being partly reintegrated in the capitalization ratio by the central banks of the major financial centers – depend crucially on highly reliable advanced technology: it must be determined to what extent the control of a communications satellite would mean a decisive technological edge for the firm able to use it. And in personal banking, where individuals' needs for financial products and related items (leisure activities, insurance) will tend to become worldwide over the next ten years, is the handling of clients' business improved by using a communications satellite? If so, for what reasons? Finally, given that the two principal market segments (large corporate accounts and individuals) and products (such as credit cards, swaps, etc.) are growing at an exponential rate around the world, the global bank enterprise needs a highly specified internal information-gathering and processing system.

Is the communications satellite, then, a privileged tool? Must a spider's-web system be designed with a communications satellite at its centre, linked to different decentralized modules spread across the world? Drawing on the logics of office technology, of telecommunications and/or aerospace, and of capital goods suppliers, the strategic evolution of global banks will inevitably go through a phase of satellite development.

Communications satellites The technological constraints to which the large organizations of the future will be subject will be, to a large extent, determined by the evolution of telecommunications satellites.

The setting-up of a space telecommunications system involves operating costs – in addition to the investment cost – totaling annually about 10 percent of the amount of the investment and the cost of the earth-based segment. Construction costs vary from one system to the next: $35 m–$60 m for a satellite of the traditional type (864 MHz capacity, 24 C-band repeaters, etc.), $60 m–$100 m for a satellite placed in orbit, and $250 m–$300 m for a system of three satellites, one in reserve on the ground and two in orbit.

Over the past twenty years telecommunications satellites have fulfilled specific functions in telecommunications networks; they have also extended the range of services offered and enabled new firms to enter the market.[3] Their function in the decades to come will depend on the evolution of telecommunications space sytems. Technical progress will in all likelihood involve:

- the relationships which link the modulation of signals and access to the satellite;
- the frequencies used, that is, the targeting of the transmission;
- the available power and the satellite's mass.

The economic performance of satellites[4] will be linked to their life-span, their weight, their volume, and their capacity: all areas in which technological progress has been achieved.

The repeater is the most important element of the satellite, containing the amplifiers and oscillators through which the signal is amplified and conveyed so that there is no interference between the ascending and descending paths. The technology has evolved over the past twenty years: progressive wave tubes now offer not only better amplification but also greater realiability and longer life; the satellites are lighter in weight;

and C-band solid state amplifiers have made their appearance. Improvements in the use of energy, both mechanical and electrical, have made it possible to extend the life of satellites and increase their available power; and the extension in on-board processing and increases in capacity offer greater load-carrying potential. However, even though average satellite life-expectancy rose in the early 1970s from seven to eight, then to ten years and power from 600 W to 1–1.5 kW, there are still problems relating to commutation and regeneration on board of the transmitted signals.

Future generations of satellites are expected to allow commutation between descending repeaters and beams. Other modes of commutation will depend on the introduction of on-board regeneration of signals, that is, each signal being demodulated, processed, then remodulated. The aim of this operation is to improve the quality of transmission while achieving a minimum conjunction of errors on the ascending and descending routes.

The next technological achievements will involve intersatellite connections. Even if economies of scale favored the choice of large platforms with multiple missions, reliability factors could still favor the cluster of satellites instead. Also in favor of such intersatellite connections are considerations of continuous service (the need for emergency capacities in case of failure) and flexible reconfiguration of networks (the flexibility of space systems enabling satellites to change their orbital position with ease). The necessary conditions for the accumulation of this capital (partial replacement of failing capacities, minimization of immobilized capital, required flexibility of systems) lead to the conclusion that satellite evolution will follow the modular route.

Evidently, satellites are a long way from technological maturity. Future progress in this area will determine not only the different types of traffic (international traffic, domestic private traffic, public and high-range traffic, teleconferences, office technology, etc.), but also the major types of applications: on the one hand, traditional traffic (telephone and equivalent operations), and transcontinental traffic, on the other hand, wide-band or high-flow traffic, including the transmission of television programmes and digital flows from office equipment.

Expert systems The specific contribution to banking of technological progress can be further illustrated by the opportunities offered by expert systems.[5]

Theoretically defined as computer programs based on a compilation of expertise accumulated in a given profession which are capable of simulating that expertise, expert systems constitute the most direct application of artificial intelligence and, consequently, differ from conventional programs in the following respects:[6]

- the capacity to solve complex problems;
- heuristic reasoning processes using principles of approximation which often make up the body of expert know-how;
- the capacity to pose pertinent questions in a language close to human language;
- manipulation and reflection using more symbols than descriptive numerical data;
- the possibility of reasoning on the basis of incomplete data;
- the capacity to explore several hypotheses simultaneously.

These characteristics give them the following advantages;

- greater ease in the maintenance and extension of their application due to the separation between the conceptual infrastructure and the processor;
- easier dialog between the machine and the user on account of the almost natural language of the processor;
- a more attractive development of language learning and representation than in traditional systems.

In practice, expert systems represent that generation of computers meant to simulate human reasoning with the help of a basis of knowledge and logical procedures, generally referred to as an 'inference motor'. These systems open up new possibilities, such as:

- the processing of symbolic, non-quantitative data;

- the solving of problems which are beyond mathematical and/ or simple algorithmic models;
- the capacity to represent the stages of a mental process, so as to explain the choice procedures and to justify conclusions.

Like any human expert, expert systems integrate all available information, even if incomplete or uncertain, in their reasoning. The system chooses from the plausible hypotheses and looks for possible solutions using empirical or heuristic rules derived from the accumulation of knowledge in the profession concerned, once key factors have been identified and conceptualized. The usefulness of these systems to banking is considerable: diagnosis, detection of errors, interpretation and processing of complex data, accounting reports, planning. This includes the banker's traditional industrial activities which require wide knowledge and permanently sustained judgment capacities based on solid professional experience. There is no shortage of areas of application:[7] instantaneous financial analysis in the evaluation of significant evolutionary factors, assistance in marketing, design of credit files, portfolio management, management of cash in foreign currencies, monitoring of risk, accounting, and information supply and processing generally.

This potential justifies giving priority to formation of an integrated approach to expert systems. Implementation of these systems will be a long-term process and the success of the banking firm that adopts them will depend on the strategy of implementation, which must be thoroughly elaborated and closely monitored.

Technology's implications for the evolution of banking

Once adopted – assuming the choices were judicious ones – technology has a positive effect on the bank's profits by directly modifying its cost function, either through increasing productivity or simply by modifying the cost function itself, thus making the combination of factors more efficient.[8] Acting in this way simultaneously on costs and earnings, technology has become the major strategic element in a sector that recent structural changes have condemned to a (temporary) drop in profitability. Moreover, recent measures to reinforce equity, deregulation (which has enabled non-bank enterprises to acquire particularly lucrative market shares), and the high level of provision resulting from the default of high-leveraged debtors and developing-country risks have reduced the average rate of return on equity in the sector, which, as indicated in a recent survey of thirty-five banks regularly monitored by Salomon Brothers, fell from 15.5 percent in 1979 to 13.2 percent in 1984. This drop in average earnings, combined with the decline in the profit rate, has depressed the internal capital formation rate which, having stood at 10 percent in 1979 and 1980, is now down to around a mere 7 percent.

Under these conditions, the introduction of technology is inevitably imperative, and this is reflected in the amount of funds banks are devoting to it.

Banking costs and products Technology, as we have seen, both modifies existing product costs and also helps create new products.[9] Not only has it modified the cost of handling private individuals, but it has changed the very nature of these costs. Indeed, thanks to technology, the entry cost to account management for individuals has plummeted for industrial or commercial firms, which can now set up various types of information management systems within their own establishments. Not so very long ago the building infrastructure cost was a significant entry barrier. Now it is possible for any institution which, from a regulatory point of view, fulfills the required conditions and in addition possesses the required systems, to serve individuals at a relatively low marginal cost by using existing distribution networks. Petrol stations and supermarkets are examples. This lowering of entry barriers has also seen the emergence in the US, and more recently in the United Kingdom and continental Europe, of significant players from the industrial or distribution sectors, such as Marks & Spencer, General Motors, Peugeot, and Sears.

The cost reduction is all the greater because technology and information can never be dissociated. Such a separation is certainly impossible in banking matters, as the evolution of risk assessment of individuals attests. In his traditional role, the bank manager assessed the financial capacity of each household. The need for a bank manager to assess a customer's credit-worthiness individually has been replaced by systems which contain all the relevant information required to reach a credit decision, via a process which is largely statistical. In this way the information/technology duplex fundamentally calls into question branch networks and the ways in which they function.

The principal banking products revolutionized by technology are the money-market products. To effect arbitrage a trader who trades between these products has real-time price feeds and a knowledge of what is happening throughout the world and is able to benefit from market price differences by analyzing the prices and other information on on-line systems.

In the individual banking sector, technology has conquered all aspects of card operations[10] and fund movements, thanks to the radical modification in the management of customers' accounts and finances. The impact of technology in the foreseeable future, for households at least, will be on two types of products: data-transmission and money-flow products, increasing the capacity to move money and information ever more rapidly and easily, using the automatic teller and the card, to obtain information on accounts, to give banking instructions, or to pay suppliers.

The decrease in costs resulting from technological progress must be understood in the broader context. In most cases, and in particular for banks of a global nature, data processing does not reduce management costs in absolute terms. Reductions in personnel are in general more than offset by additional costs for the management and depreciation of the computer investment. In fact, only the unit processing cost of an operation diminishes, during a period where volumes have shown a very rapid upward trend. Moreover, it is not only a question of indirect costs – production costs and so on – but also of costs that are difficult to evaluate. Among those, security costs (frauds, thefts, counterfeit operations, etc.) must be given particular attention. Indeed, in the current phase of data-processing activity, there is an increased risk of fraud; preventive means lag behind fraudulent techniques of manipulating files, gaining access to the central computer, etc., and to this must be added the difficulty of engaging the services of computer teams on a permanent basis and the relative underdevelopment of computer auditing. The current situation, of course, varies considerably depending on the nature of the bank and of its products, sources, and transactions.

In this context it is interesting to note the development of the "smart card" which benefited from contributions made by biometry.[11] Diagramatically, a "smart" identification card has five zones: a secret code identification zone, a memory zone, a functional zone recording the data which are the basis of identification procedures, a free zone, and an industrial zone intended for the identification of the user and the manufacturer respectively. Technological evolution has enabled gradual integration of the smart card in the field of biometric identification. The use of authentication systems based on the recognition of a number of identifications remains insufficient, whereas the memory capacity of the smart card and the complete protection of zones enables it to have its own identification system. New technologies use biometry – fingerprints, voice analysis – when the user maintains his or her natural voice. On automatic teller machines (ATMs), the use of a voice is not, however, possible because of background noise. There are, however, other methods, such as the breathing rate, that could be used, and these could overcome the failings of the plastic card (often lost or stolen) and the signature (only verifiable *ex post facto*). Future technologies will offer greater precision by relying on identification of eyelashes or eyes without the removal of glasses, for example. Even better, some biometric research suggests that each individual gives off a ray which delineates his or her space of existence, and that this can be detected and used as subject of personal identification.

Without anticipating how far ahead these innovations are in practical terms, it is already possible to see the advantages offered by improved banker identification of customers. First, the parties tend to become involved personally, therefore personally responsible and consequently avoid errors. Secondly, the recognized existence of a personal identification system is a powerful dissuader from fraud, both by the user and by the bank employee.

A bank's choice of systems will be determined by numerous parameters such as its anticipated growth, replacement requirements, and maintenance and cost considerations.

Investments and modes of competition Assessing the effect of technological progress on competition also involves analyzing the effects of investment costs on the evolution of market structures.[12] The scale of investments in the technical domain is such that one can legitimately wonder about the barriers to competition which technology costs will erect. The problem of the investment level varies, however, according to the market leaders. Industrial firms which have already created an information technology network to manage their customer accounts or inventory flow can, with only a low incremental investment, produce and manage financial assets and/or services at competitive prices and in a short period of time. In contrast, banks, forced by competition and the requirements of their customers to renew their investments in information technology, must bear considerable marginal costs, both for the development and implementation of new investments over a period from two to five years, and simultaneously for the management of the existing infrastructure. This includes the cost of reducing and/or renovating existing human and property infrastructure – particularly high in Europe and Japan, where social legislation and practices are well established.

In the current state of the market, it will probably be network banks that will have to make the largest investments.

We can begin to measure the expense of technology by looking at how its share in non-financial charges has evolved. Banking devotes a larger share of its non-financial charges to investment in automation than any other industry – except for the computer industry itself. For the world's thirty or so largest banks, this share currently stands at between 11 percent and 15 percent, after an explosive increase in recent years. It doubled in the 1970s and 1980s and prospects for growth are still significant for the present decade.

More precisely, 2–3 percent of these non-financial expenses are devoted to communications. This is an area in which growth is fostered by the intensification of upstream competition as a result of deregulation in the telecommunications sector. Between 35 percent and 40 percent of expenditure on automation is allocated to the creation of new systems or to the improvement of existing systems.

Nor is this tendency running out of momentum; on the contrary, continued expansion is called for on at least three counts: first, and above all, technology reduces labor input in the banking sector; secondly, by introducing new products, it enables whoever adopts it to be present on the new markets which demand advanced production processes; and thirdly, it alters the practice of several banking functions, for example the money-market activities,[13] cash management and traditional banking operations for private individuals, small- and medium-sized firms, and global firms.

This turn to technology, targeting a well-defined product line, will enable banks to become more profitable than other kinds of business. Nevertheless, this choice must be part of a proactive long-term strategy, not a reactive or fragmented strategy born of a defensive attitude that the evolution of market structures will make more and more perilous – as indicated already in the competitive reports of banks and non-bank financial institutions. The non-integrated strategy risks allowing non-bank enterprises to fill the gaps left open by the banks.

Depending on the technological choices made, two categories of large network banks will come to coexist:

- those having made the right choices, attracting the consumers and companies to whom they will offer products and services at competitive prices, thanks to economies of scale and consequently with lower processing and marketing costs;
- those which have backed away from the transformation in structures and in people, the high investment costs, and the complexity inherent in highly sophisticated integrated systems.

As a result, the banking system characterized by this dual structure will undergo yet further concentration as the weak are bought out by the strong.

Such a split seems all the more likely when one notes that the large amounts of capital that banks need to raise in order to carry out these technological investments is already forcing the smaller ones to choose between extreme specialization, going under, or subcontracting. The establishment of a global system for funds transfer costs a minimum of $25 m–$50 m and a complete global credit card system $50 m–$100 m, while an integrated world exchange money-market and trading activities system can represent an investment of $100 m–$200 m. For the large network banks, the development of all the modules required to manage the activities of individuals, in real time and in an integrated manner, represents a capital outlay of the order of $1 bn, to which must be added the cost of converting the existing infrastructure. This represents, depending on the country, an additional cost varying from 50 percent to 100 percent.[14] Taking into account the sums at stake, it will be agreed that few banks have the critical mass necessary to be present simultaneously in all sectors.

The size of the technological investment[15] cannot be separated from the geographical spread of investment required of a global financial institution. Here too, the estimated amounts and risks are considerable. For a European bank, a significant presence in the United States in two of the three fundamental sectors, i.e., merchant banking, money-market activities, and personal banking, represents an investment in the region of $500 m–$1 bn. Taking into account exchange parities, market size, and current stock-market prices, a strategic investment in Japan will probably call for comparable sums. Few large British, American, Japanese, and West German banks have invested or plan to invest on this scale. An even greater obstacle than the financial demands to the implementation of a successful global strategy lies in the need for staff and managers thoroughly versed in these technologies.

Those institutions which succeed in marshaling the finance and the expertise to mount a credible global strategy will see their profits leap on account of a dominant market share in the processing of flows (the privileged position of the large counterparts) and the capacity to write off considerable investments over greater volumes of activities.

TECHNOLOGICAL PROGRESS IN THE VARIOUS AREAS OF BANKING

The impact of technology on banking will be enormous. It will mean not only profound changes in the conditions of production and competition in banking but also an upheaval in all the areas of banking.

The basic areas of banking

There is no one classification of banking activities. Among the numerous ones on offer is that frequently adopted in the English-language literature,[16] in which the activities fall into five main segments:

1. the commercial department, including traditional commercial activities and corporate accounts;
2. personal banking, including the whole range of services and products offered to households;
3. activities involving clearing, movements of funds, and information;
4. all the operations linked to risk assets;
5. investment, trading, and arbitrage activities, grouped together under the term of money-market activities, including asset and liability management.

Risk

There are various ways of assessing and measuring counterparty risk. In some cases (for example, groups of individual borrowers) it is possible to use historical data on defaults. But these techniques should not be used in the same way for determining the risk for small and medium-sized firms.

From the point of view of risk, counterparties typically fall into one of the following three categories:

(1) Individuals with a long enough history to provide historical data which will enable the bank to assess future risk on the basis of past experience, subject to certain periodic or circumstantial adjustments.

(2) The large private or public sectors, which generate risks principally of a strategic and/or political nature. This market segment includes developing countries attempting to reschedule their debts as well as multinational companies in industry, finance, or services, central banks, and international organizations. The main features are:

a The risks are either geopolitical, or geostrategic. Only a few American, European, and Japanese banks can assess the first kind of requisite risk; only a few Japanese and West German banks have the internal facilities and have forged the privileged links with the leading industrial firms that enable accurate assessment of risks of a geostrategic nature.

b The sector's banking needs are principally related to trading activities, which are all the more complex given the abundance of liquid assets, and the management of flows and data. Service activities, such as mergers, acquisitions, and complex financing packages for exports and foreign locations have lagged far behind, although recently their importance has grown.

(3) The final category comprises all other customers. It groups together, with the exception of private individuals and large organizations, all the counterparties forming the thread of a country's economic fabric who do not always have direct and automatic access to financial markets, but who, on account of their rapid growth, are heavy consumers of credit. This market segment is essentially comprised of family or personal undertakings. It is a sector where the failure rate is often high and where the risks taken by the banks as lenders are far from negligible. The bank must have skilled representatives in the

field, capable of assessing situations and making the right decisions, because assessing in order to decide whether to accept these clients' risks demands especially good judgment. It is noteworthy that this sector seems to be the least favored by many banks, because results depend on efforts sustained over decades, in sharp contrast to the gains from money-market activities which are often immediate; furthermore, the real risks are more often than not greater than the statistical risks on loans to individuals. Yet the industrial health of a country requires that this sector receive a professional service and commitment of the highest quality. The service to this segment has a relatively low technological content and draws its inspiration to a much greater extent from the banker's traditional roles as a source of information and as a countervailing force, encouraging successful initiatives and keeping a check on the client's attempts to take excessive risks.

TECHNOLOGICAL PROGRESS AND THE RANGE OF BANKING PRODUCTS

Segment products: Electronic funds transfer[17]

Electronic funds transfer remains one of the most important technological innovations, taking into account its effects on the proliferation of banking products and on the improvement of existing banking techniques. A description of the current state of technology in this area and the prospects for evolution of the payment system will enable us to identify possible strategic orientations in the decades ahead.

Payment systems,[18] considered as a series of links between banks, on the one hand, and between banks and their traditional clients – households and companies – on the other, are based, in all industrialized countries, on two kinds of support:

- an electronic support which is more and more frequently employed;
- a paper support which is already a tool of the past.

Although present-day studies devoted to the impact of technology on the banking system focus on cash dispensers, automatic bank tellers, point-of-sale terminals, and home banking services, banks will be forced to continue using paper-based systems as well until a gradual transformation of existing links has been completed. When these become entirely electronic, a generalized electronic transfer system will undoubtedly be set up.

At the time of writing, direct electronic communications do not exist between the principals and the automatic clearing houses, though they are likely to be set up in several financial centers by 1992. Furthermore, banks use magnetic tapes to process banking operations with most customers, whereas the clearing house is automated. Therefore, within the payment system, only certain links are electronic, principally the following two kinds:

1 Automatic dispensers, point-of-sale terminals, and home deposits link small customers to bank branches by means of an electronic system. Similar links exist between important customers and the clearing house which operate without any intermediary. The bank branches, the clearing house, the communication center, and the other national banks are also electronically linked to one another.
2 Automated international interbank links (the Chaps system in London), eliminating all paper for fund movements, have been developed on a very extensive basis. Automation began approximately fifteen years ago with the Swift system, followed by the Chips system in New York.

All the other links in the payment system – those between bank branches and head office, between the head office and the central bank, between the central bank and the banks of other countries – still use paper-based systems. The introduction of the electronic transfer system clearly involves a process of transforming the banking business[19] as well as providing a generalized method of handling payment operations.

Creating reference products

Institutions and individuals

Given these conditions, what is the current state of technological innovation in this sector?

The new products will not have the same impact for institutions and individuals, which, as was noted above, constitute two distinct segments. It would be interesting to assess the transformations induced by technological progress in the separate but linked areas of costs on the one hand and products/individuals/institutions on the other. The points of intermediation thus obtained could then be interpreted as reference points of the technological constraint. The effects of technological progress in terms of the costs of services offered to individuals focus on the actual nature of those costs. Hence, any institution can now lower its cost of entry to the individuals' account management business if it has a computer system with integrated software, terminals, and access to captive customers.

This cost factor explains the entry into the banking sector of supermarkets, petrol stations, and automobile manufacturers in America, Europe, and Japan. The obsolescence of capital, accelerated by new technology, leads to maintenance and, especially, renewal costs. This 'functional depreciation' introduces a new cost element – which, given the scale of the requirements of the innovations concerned, is a very considerable one.

The new products currently offered to households are confined to data-transmission and money-flow products improving the circulation of information and funds: automatic teller machines, credit cards, visual support hardware such as the minitel network, investment products, and automatic credit facilities. Even video technology can be integrated into these products, and the relationship of information and funds flow between the banker and his customer will tend to take the route of the visual image. Eventually this technology will give the individual access to money-market activities hitherto confined to large corporations.

These considerations could apply to all the activities of a branch network of the domestic bank. That would mean, ultimately, restructuring traditional branches and modifying their functions.

The trend toward branch concentration appears as inescapable as the redefinition of their mission. It is reasonable to predict, though, that not all the bank's functions will be susceptible to automation. The banking relationship will not be limited to operating accounts and buying and selling certain products. On the one hand, banks will tend to increase their range of services; on the other, personal relationships will retain special importance in many cases. The restructuring of branch networks will have to take account of the need for individually tailored advice for a small number of private customers as well as for small, medium-sized, and large firms which will pay for these services at their true price. In many cases, there is also a close interrelationship between cash management and business development in small and medium-sized firms. The pooling of these functions in selected branches throughout the country, equipped with specialist staff and the appropriate technology, would satisfy an important customer need and have considerable added value.

New data-transmission techniques will enable individuals to manage their banking relationship as they see fit, without any time constraint. The scope of these innovations will be even greater if they act on the relationships between banking institutions and individuals.[20]

Transformations within the banking system

These will be based on two major innovations: teller terminals and interbank electronic links.[21] It is already known that the functions of teller terminals do not differ very much from those fulfilled by automatic tellers: cash dispensing, acceptance of deposits, and account operations. However, teller terminals can also be programed to perform a large number of calculations involving annual instalments, exchange rates, insurance premiums, etc. In addition to these technological advantages, they reduce costs by considerably increasing work productivity, limiting the running time of certain operations, and avoiding the accumulation of administrative tasks. Electronic links will be improved both between the different banks and within the banks themselves.

The commutation center, which is used for automatic tellers and other points of sale when the operations in question involve several participating banks, constitutes the first electronic automated system. The Chips (New York) and Chaps (London) networks can be included in the same category of innovation. On account of their specialization and their limitation to a minimum volume of transactions, they do not yet constitute perfect systems. In fact, none of the existing interbank electronic networks to date allows the direct inclusion of operations from other banks – automatic tellers and points-of-sale terminals being, of course, exceptions to the rule.

Generalizing automation, consequently, depends more on the ability to build interbank links than it does on the development of technological innovations. A truly generalized system will invalidate the distinction between periodic payments and occasional payments, large settlements and settlements of a small amount, in the sense that it will effect all operations instantaneously.

Still better, automatic teller machines, benefiting from the improved power of microcomputers, will, when central units "go down", be able to continue recording banking operations on cassette tapes, thus enabling service to continue. Ultimately, once an expert system is integrated, they will be able to effect all funds transfers by themselves.

Banks and their private customers

We have already referred to the sea-change in this area in the context of automatic teller machines, point-of-sale terminals, and domestic bank installations. Indeed, it was cash dispensers which were the first innovations in the automation of banking services; since then, little by little, they have undergone improvements. Originally restricted to payment of a fixed sum, the system has come to offer greater flexibility in the amount to be withdrawn and then to provide a variety of other services. Automatic teller machines today take cash and cheque deposits, display statements of current payments, accept requests for account statements to be mailed, and even perform transfers from one account to another. In other words, automatic teller machines provide most of the routine services offered by a bank, including buying and selling securities and granting credit allowances, either by granting an overdraft or by using a credit card – with the exception of periodic transactions such as payments at regular intervals, which are subject to particular provisions and procedures.

The multiplicity of services performed by automatic teller machines, particularly in places such as hospitals, factories, and universities, has inevitably led banks to co-operate among themselves. In the particular case of automatic teller machines, educating the public will be a determining factor in their use. Indeed, even if the introduction of expert systems leads to a significant decrease in their price, it will nevertheless remain high, because of the large number of mechanical elements involved.

The development of automatic teller machines is part of a long-term trend. In the future, point-of-sale terminals will be developed even further. These terminals,[22] set up in supermarkets or at other points of sale, operate with cards which effect instantaneous transfer of funds from the customer's account to the shopkeeper's. In the beginning, pilot schemes were limited to verifying the customer's provision of cheques or accepting their credit cards. These experiments encountered numerous failures, probably because of the promoters' impatience with public resistance to changing habits: heavy investments in terminals and telecommunications had to be made, and profitability depended on a sufficient number of customers using these facilities. In other words, adoption of point-of-sale terminals hangs on the advantages they offer to consumers and shopkeepers. In fact, consumers seem to obtain more benefits than shopkeepers: whereas lower risks of theft and deferred payment constitute substantial advantages, shopkeepers in many cases still prefer cash. However, it is important for them to see a reduction in the risks of theft at the cash register as well as in paperwork management costs.

Finally, home banking originated in the United States to facilitate the payment of bills by telephone. Automation, promoted initially by savings institutions and then by banks, consisted first in making keyboard telephones available to customers, and especially by introducing the videotext.

Videotext systems, using the display function of the television set and telephone lines, enable the consumer to enter into direct contact not only with banks, but also with travel agencies, airline companies or department stores. They allow, of course, transfer of funds by telephone, pioneered by Verbraucherbank in West Germany. The complexity of the computer access system is largely offset by the multiplicity of services offered, including bank statements, ordering check books, checking interest rates on financial markets, credit limits, available balance; transferring money to a third party, term investment, money order dispatching – and even sending messages of a general nature to the bank. Among all these functions, the information one has been used more widely than the transfer one.

In conclusion, the consumer-oriented electronic banking services have spread relatively slowly due to the size of the investment required by the banks on the one hand, and the very gradual evolution of consumer habits on the other.

Regardless of technical progress, we can identify three major trends in home banking. First, the slow pace of its adoption could pick up momentum through increased use of services such as ordering merchandise or reserving tickets for travel or entertainment. Better still, given the shortcomings of the mail, low-cost electronic transfer of information could replace post office mail. Here, it provides the more efficient service which threatens the less efficient with extinction.

Secondly, these innovations could accelerate the demolition of barriers within the financial services sector by allowing non-bank organizations with computer networks identical to those of banks to compete with them in their own sector.

Finally, the development of home banking will obviously limit the expansion of branches and lead a certain number of institutions to rethink their network's role, mission, and way of operating.

TECHNOLOGICAL PROGRESS AND THE FUTURE OF BANKING

Adapting existing products: The new intermediation

The best managed banks' strategy solves the problems posed by the fall in the sector's profitability by segmenting their activities along product lines. Using the gross price margin variable as a yardstick, profit objectives demand a forward-looking view which incorporates technology into a well-chosen line of products.[23] But evaluation of a given product line's profitability depends on reliable information – as do all management control systems based on performance measurement.

Technology intervenes in the provision of services such as execution of payments for firms, consolidation of cash surpluses, and investment of these funds in a constantly growing range of instruments. It offers ever greater comparative advantage by enabling the most efficient exploitation possible of investment possibilities on a global level.

The new services resulting from the introduction of technology and from which the banking business can reap sizeable profits include:

- verification and control of the day's debits and credits, allowing firms to adjust their cash flow on a daily basis and make investment choices on the basis of highest return within corporate policy guidelines;
- cross-checking of accounts, ensuring up-to-date book-keeping;
- daily electronic transfer of funds;

- minimization of transactions resulting from the number of transfers between companies or between companies and consumers;
- traditional deposit activity and associated services: codification of checks, endorsement, creation of microfilms;
- use of terminals, entry of transactions on to personal computers via the central processing unit;
- cash-management assistance programs;
- for industrial customers, use of the bank's communications network as an alternative to private communications networks.

In this sector of cash management, the competitive factors, which when mastered confer a comparative advantage, are: the quality of the operators and the network to which they belong; the development of new product lines; marketing; and the performance of decision and management support tools.

Cash management appears to be one of the key areas of the banking business and it is crucial to its profitability. However, the size of the investments required to install telecommunications systems capable of offering differentiated services restricts its profitability to large banks which have considerable financial resources and the ability to attract and retain experienced and talented operators. In this area, technological transformation must be accompanied by major changes in management methods, in particular with regard to the delegation of authority and control.

Another sector likely to be profoundly transformed by new technologies is that of securities management and maintenance: interest and dividend payments, transactions involving shares, options, and other marketable securities, monitoring of investment performances, settlement and payment operations, and the production of analysis reports.

In all these areas, the factors of success are for the most part technology-related.

Creating new activities: Toward banking by visual image

Technological innovation in telecommunications satellites and expert systems increases the possibility of audiovisual communication. As technology improves funds and information transmission, it is reasonable to expect television to be gradually introduced in banking and to modify both internal management methods and relationships with customers.[24] Indeed, a situation could be envisaged in which general economic advice and information, or the performance report for certain types of financial assets, would be provided by video. Video recording would enable customers to store the data transmitted by their bank.

Even a rough estimate of the cost of international transmission systems shows that such systems require sizeable investment. However, the consequences of technological innovation are not limited solely to the use of more or less complex media. They also concern financial innovations.

Progress in information technology and data processing has enabled financial engineers and traders to evaluate in real time the comparative advantages of new assets with complex financial structures. These improvements have simultaneously enabled a more discriminating evaluation of certain risks and, consequently, the implementation of hedging methods suitable for certain types of market. In addition, the major reduction in transmission costs and the expansion of telecommunications networks have created a global financial market on which agents of financial innovation can contact final users and, thus, encourage more and more financial institutions to participate actively in these new financial markets.

Finally, improvement of transmission flows has probably helped to eliminate profitable monopolies and has created competitive price structures in traditional sectors, thus encouraging financial institutions to pursue innovation with even greater intensity. The wide dissemination of market information on screens has reduced the costs of searching for a competitive price system, a cost reduction which has resulted in lower margins on traditional operations. Also, banks are forced to create new, customized products, enabling, at least in the take-off phase, sizeable margins to be made.

2

◇

The Competition Constraint

◆

COMPETITION: THE BACKGROUND

Structure, conduct, performance: The logic of concentration

In the study of competition, industry is traditionally divided into two large groups:

1 The atomistic industries, where the concentration of suppliers is very low, their number very high, and their market share particularly low, so that any attempt at discretionary variance of quantity or price will be unimportant to other firms within the industry.
2 The oligopolistic industries where concentration is strong. These are markets where each of the small number of producers holds an important share of the market and thus sees it as sensitive to price or quantity behavior: any modification of either variable leads to a change in the level of market price or the quantities produced (or exchanged).

Firms' conduct will vary depending on whether they are oligopolistic or atomistic.[1]

Atomistic suppliers consider price a fixed element and produce the quantities which will maximize profit.[2] Any concerted action by groups of firms is precluded by the sheer number of players and their compulsion to break all collusive agreements, without, however, necessarily triggering a competitive response. Indeed, such a violation, because of the fragmentation of markets, would probably have no effect.

In an oligopolistic structure, on the other hand, each supplier holds a significant share of the market and knows that his activities will influence market prices. Consequently, he will anticipate his rivals' reactions. Their restricted number will permanently maintain the temptation to collude to exercise collective control over quantity and prices. The interdependence of decisions automatically creates a climate where various strategies are deployed.

Hence, within an oligopolistic structure, differences in market and concentration models seem to result from differences in the conduct and performance of producers. Whatever the case, the theory sets down two laws: (1) *ceteris paribus*, oligopolistic interdependence grows as the concentration becomes stronger; (2) the greater this concentration, the more strongly firms are tempted to adopt a strategy of joint profit maximization. The reciprocals of the two laws also apply.

A wide range of markets can be considered potential oligopolies.[3] Indeed, in cases where market shares are allocated in a way that creates interdependence, there exists an oligopoly. Within oligopolies, we can distinguish subdivisions defined according to the concentration model and the conduct of firms. Structural interdependence means that:

1 Any firm operating in an oligopoly is tempted to enter into collusion with its competitors in order to determine the quantity/price vector which ensures that the whole group maximizes profit. This, logically, would ensure all members a maximum dividend.
2 At the same time, that firm feels the desire to increase its share of the cumulative profit to the detriment of the other firms, even if it sometimes means sacrificing the total amount of joint profit. It will therefore often be tempted to act in isolation on prices and quantities.

Consequently, each firm suffers an internal conflict between the strategies of joint profit maximization and independent profit maximization.[4] The actual strategy chosen will be some sort of compromise. The structure of the oligopoly, and in particular the degree and model of concentration, will determine conduct and performance. Theoretically, under certain conditions, no firm in an oligopoly gains by undertaking an isolated strategy. These conditions are principally the following:

1 the number of suppliers is limited, creating strong interdependence recognized by all the competitors;
2 their market shares for a given market price are equal;
3 their cost conditions are identical;
4 any variation in prices or quantities is immediately known by the others.

If these conditions are not met – and in reality they are not – individual firms have a thousand reasons to attempt independent and antagonistic strategies.

Ultimately, there are two aspects of concentration that influence the outcome of the conflict between the joint maximization strategy and the strategy of independence.[5] They are the degree of supplier concentration, expressed in terms of the number of suppliers and individual market shares, and the presence or absence of a band of small suppliers[6] in the oligopolistic industry and its quantitative importance. This last consideration calls for some clarification. A pocket of small suppliers, without any power over the market, can destabilize the prices established by the large firms in an oligopolistic industry. The difference in the situations of the few large firms on the one hand and the numerous small ones on the other means that each group must operate in a completely independent way.

The problem of concentration is also linked to the sector's efficiency and consequently to the efficiency of the entire economic system. The search for maximum profits involves minimizing costs and seeking an optimal economic structure (organization).[7]

Concentration, competition, and the place of banks in the economy

For a very long time, the banking sector remained relatively stable.[8] There were few new entrants and market shares were stable. This resulted in profit levels being maintained. However, new factors have come into play, such as the emergence of new competitors, regulatory changes, and, finally, the international debt crisis. It is to these current problems that we shall now turn.

Only a few years ago, defining the nature of the banking system was not difficult:[9] it was a group of institutions with well-defined characteristics. Ten years from now, such a definition will have become, to a large extent, obsolete. Indeed, bank products and those involved in banking will be so diversified that a new definition will have to account for this very heterogeneity. The bank – or rather, its financial activities – will comprise a set of services carried out by a variety of institutions and organizations from the most diverse areas of economic activity.

These transformations of the banking world mean that selecting the right strategy will be critical.

Not so long ago, mention of the revolutionary changes to be brought about by technology in the serene world of banking was considered futuristic. The speed of the technological revolution, however, forced banks to transform themselves at their own expense. Among the comparative advantages swept away by technology was the banks' exclusive monopoly on a set of operations.

Nevertheless the banks' social importance has been maintained, indeed fostered, for some time. Several factors have contributed to this.

There is a rapidly growing gap between the real economy of goods and services and the financial economy. International trade represents approximately \$3,000 bn a year; spot and forward exchange operations, including futures, performed on a daily basis amount to approximately 50–75 percent of this sum. The participation of an increasingly large number of firms and skilled individuals in the management of financial flows, owes probably less to any social function than to a propensity to gamble which may have, on the contrary, a corrosive effect on general economic behavior and on a country's ability to create lasting wealth. The current pre-eminence of the financier over the industrialist could be the expression of a multidimensional social phenomenon, namely, the desire to slow down the rate of change in relationships of power and in the thinking and working habits involved in the implementation of any productive investment, as well as the desire to consume and enjoy rather than to accumulate wealth beyond current levels. This reflects the relative maladjustment of the Western cultural model based on individualism, a binary mode of thinking, and a weakening of the desire for world pre-eminence (which privileges the long term) in favor of the pursuit of pleasure which accords greater value to the present at a time when industrial positionings often demand commitments ranging anywhere from fifteen to twenty-five years.

These factors could account for the explosion in the financial industry which is reflected by the relative importance of speculation, that is to say trading activities, which have *no links with commercial transactions*.

All these changes have repercussions on the behavior of the various players which the banker will have to take into account. He or she needs to know whether individuals pay in cash, by check, or via electronic money, with the assistance of home computers or a telephone, or at points of sale at supermarkets; whether they borrow money traditionally in bank branches, by automatic request, by credit card, or on the basis of margins defined from their stock portfolio; and whether companies choose a bank loan or a loan on the market. These sociological, behavioral, financial and technological transformations are very closely interwoven.

ANALYZING BANKING COMPETITION: THE INTENSITY AND THE MEANS

The evolution of competition in the banking sector will be determined by the market share of each of the large banks in different segments and geographical regions. The intensity and the means of competition lead us to choose segmentation by institution: states, firms, individuals, and financial organizations.

Analysis by institutional segmentation: States, companies, individuals

In the case of credit aids to countries with serious foreign debt problems, the high degree of risk to be assumed forces the banks, at a certain level, to collaborate instead of engaging in traditional competition. For the others, today's trends are converging toward greater security for debts. In the case of states that are economically weak or that are having serious difficulties in meeting foreign payments,[10] the international banking organizations, the states, their central banks, and the private international banks join together to assume collectively a risk that is both considerable and difficult to quantify; and in respect of which it is becoming increasingly clear that given the lack of an institutional framework and of the requisite political will, most of the debt will have to be written off.[11]

As far as companies are concerned, any analysis must differentiate between small firms and multinational corporations.

What is noteworthy with regard to the small firms segment is the comparative advantage of regional banks and/or banks that operate in a truly decentralized way, and certain suppliers who benefit from direct experience of their clients' working methods and in evaluating their customers' technical worth, and which are therefore able to reach more accurate assessments of risk. The regional bank, because of its close contact with the client company, has inside knowledge. In addition, small and medium-sized firms are maintaining increasingly closer ties with their major customers, who, by creating financial credit sectors and providing technical and management assistance, are able to ensure intermediation profit and compete with banks in areas where they are most vulnerable, namely the goodwill of their branch network.

As far as the large companies are concerned, two factors will determine how competition evolves there: the quality of the liquidity management they offer and the ability of banks to institutionalize a relationship where all the services of an institution are mobilized to support the long-term growth strategy of the customer.

Given the importance of being able to invest and to handle market operations of a high unit amount, the three main geographical loci of competition for large corporations are Japan, which leads by a wide margin, secondly the United States and the United Kingdom, and finally Switzerland and West Germany.

Japan's emergence as principal creditor nation has reinforced the power of its financial and banking groups. At the end of 1987, Japan's short-term, foreign-held assets totalled $240 bn.[12] Since 1986, Japan has taken over from the United Kingdom as leading creditor nation.[13] The structure of the balance of payments, moreover, suggests that continued accumulation of foreign assets will make investment income the predominant item of Japan's invisibles balance.

It is generally accepted that capital flows of this size are not only significant economically but constitute a considerable asset for the world positioning of financial institutions of the country of origin. They create a monopoly that yields significant profits, comparable to that which the United Kingdom enjoyed until 1930 and to that which the United States has possessed since the end of World War II. These capital surpluses favor the competitiveness of home-country institutions not only by making available to them considerable amounts of financial resources to be managed and invested but also by enabling the development of lasting and loyal relations with the international issuer, with all that this implies in terms of profits made in other sectors ranging from merchant banking to the financing of large-scale projects.

It is interesting to note that already in April 1986, of five issues of long-term bonds by General Electric, four were managed by the Japanese.[14] Since then, Japan has become the largest single placement source of debt and equity. This is due to the enormous financial reach of their stockbrokers: Nomura's stock exchange capitalization is a multiple of Barclays's and NatWest's combined; the profits of Nomura, Daiwa, and Yamaichi are several times the profits of Citicorp, Chase, Morgan, and Bankers Trust. This pre-eminence is a direct result of a quality network, the creditor structure of the Japanese economy,[15] and by the volume of operations initiated in Japan. This will and ability to capture and to keep a dominant share of the world financial market dictates their behavior at all times.

After those in Japan, the world markets which offer attractive placement opportunities to firms are those of the United Kingdom and the United States, whose dynamism and liquidity date back some one hundred years and half a century respectively.[16] Finally, we should mention in the list of bearer markets those of Switzerland and West Germany, where liberal regulations have given operators considerable room to maneuver.

These three groups of countries,[17] by offering major placement capacities and investment opportunities to large firms, have created a new parameter in international banking competition: large firms can now benefit from these opportunities to maximize their financial gains and mobilize resources of a very diverse nature, provided that they have a credible long-term industrial strategy and operate with particularly sound judgment. In addition to the placement capacity, the establishment of an account relationship based on the bank's mobilization of all their multiproduct resources (insurance, travel, broking, hire-purchase sales, technical support, current accounts, etc.) will be a key competitive factor. To succeed with large corporate clients, banks need to be able to offer a multitude of products and, at the same time, maintain a degree of intimacy.

The third institutional sector comprises individuals. A few

important characteristics stand out here. This segment constitutes at present one of the two most profitable areas of activity and its margins can be very significant. The high level of these margins has led, as we might expect, to the entry of new firms, in particular those dealing directly with individuals, in the capacity of producer or distributor. The most convincing example – and one to which we will return – is that of the automobile industry. Car dealers, supermarket chains, and mail-order houses have gradually taken the place of banks, the financial dimension becoming both an important component of sales strategy and an additional way to improve profitability. Indeed, the extension of credit to individuals now seems to be a priority of distributors and producers who want to diversify.

Some banks have responded to this intrusion by setting up better marketing and distribution networks: Compagnie Bancaire in France, for example, or Citicorp worldwide. Other banks, like the Société Générale in France, have turned to buying hire-purchase companies in order to ensure themselves a sizeable share of the market. In the years ahead, all the indications are that in the area of consumer credit, producers and distributors will increase their market shares, because they will then be able to arbitrage, and therefore to discriminate between commercial margin and financial margin, while maximizing the two combined margins. Insurance companies, in a favorable position because of the quantity of information they hold on their customers, as well as their computer and distribution network, may also be expected to penetrate the market. In the United States and the United Kingdom, there are already an impressive number of such businesses with a wide reach, companies which have managed, despite the state of their national economies, to increase their sales turnover and their profits by granting credit at rates which defy bank competition. Competition between banks will be examined later.

For each of the four market sectors selected, it is necessary to analyze the intensity of competition and the traditional components of the marketing mix: price, product, distribution circuits, and product image. In each case, too, the banks' competitors[18] – which may be either non-bank enterprises (exogenous competition) or financial or non-financial enterprises (endogenous competition) – must also be identified.

Sovereign investors and borrowers: The rich and the poor

The primary distinction to be made in the sovereign sectors is that between those countries having difficulty repaying loans and those that are economically powerful. The nature of the institutional relationship maintained in each country between the private banks and the central bank is also important.

In most cases the domestic banks have retained entirely privileged positions within their national public domains, and the intensity of competition is accordingly still low. An exception is the United States, which, by virtue of its place in the world banking system and the financing requirements of its public deficit, has a less protected market, though even this operates under the surveillance of brokerage firms accredited by the US Treasury. Elsewhere, market shares are very stable, the rules of the game between banks being limited for the most part to fixed rules of distribution, and issue prices are largely determined by the public treasuries according to a decision-making process in which market operators participate in some form or another. Moreover, these issues are subscribed by public, semi-public, and quasi-public organizations: savings banks, insurance companies, pension funds, post offices. This world very often excludes the large international banks which still see these markets as secondary and as distributed among the domestic cartels.

The means of this competition are also defined by the public authorities: the market price, which results from supply and demand, and the administered price of money are both influenced by government intervention in the money and bond markets.[19] Governments do not seem prepared to give up their control over the issuing procedures because they want to ensure themselves a source of refinancing. Any diversification of refinancing sources will be carried out on terms which afford governments the power to approve or reject potential new participants.

Such a general tendency does not, however, rule out the existence of different situations in different countries.[20] Thus, it can be predicted that the treasury's hold on these short-, medium-, and long-term issues will be particularly tight in countries such as the United Kingdom, West Germany, France, and Italy, and will be different in the United States. The United States, of course, is set apart by virtue of the role of the dollar in the international monetary system. Financing of the American public deficit is carried out both by the American financial system and by foreign countries (especially Japan) in a vast market with numerous participants. However, all establishments authorized by the Federal Reserve to act as first-hand purchasers (primary dealers) of Treasury bonds are subject to approval and to close monitoring by the Federal Reserve. The extreme case is that of the Bank of Spain, which requires banks to prepare daily reports on the state of their transactions in negotiable instruments.

The management of sovereign assets (such as reserve assets) uses similar techniques to those employed by the financial departments of multinational firms. This offers interesting opportunities to banks which, on this front, engage in intense competition, fuelled by the overriding desire of central banks and public bodies to deal with world-size organizations in a way that enables privileged special relationships. This is the case, for example, in the discrete relationship, which is part of a long-standing tradition, between Lazard Frères and the Morgan Bank on the one hand and the Bank of France and the French, US, and UK Treasuries on the other.

The operators competing for the business of rich sovereigns are the world's leading signatures, which up until recently were only British, American, or French banks. The past few years have been notable for the emergence and success of a number of Japanese institutions. To understand this phenomenon the development of the foreign activities of Japan's commercial and long-term credit banks must be highlighted by a few figures.[21]

In 1980, only one of the world's top ten banks, measured in

terms of global assets, was Japanese; only thirteen were Japanese among the top fifty. In 1986, five (and in 1990, nine) of Japan's banks were among the top ten, and seventeen were among the top fifty. The proportion of Japanese banks' assets in the total assets of the world's ten leading banks rose from 8 percent in 1974 to 57 percent in 1987. An even better indicator is the proportion of foreign earnings in total income (interest + dividends + fees collected): steady at 15 percent throughout the end of the 1970s, it reached 47 percent at the end of 1987.[22] Official statistics of medium- and long-term loans by Japanese banks over these past ten years illustrate the growing internationalization of their balance sheet.

This expansion by Japanese banks of their international activities has been accompanied by an increasingly strong presence in London, where almost forty of them now have branches. This represents 4.5 percent of assets held in sterling, compared with less than 1 percent in 1980. Japanese banks currently account for nearly 2 percent of sterling advances and almost 20 percent of foreign currency advances to the British private and public sectors. And the percentage of their banks operating in the international loan market in London rose from 22 percent in 1980 to over 30 percent in 1987. Over the same period, their market share in new financial instruments[23] increased and doubled in the London acceptances and floating-rate notes markets – to 70 percent of the total. Also important is the increasingly significant role of the yen as an international currency. Its use in international banking credits has risen from 3.5 percent to 12 percent, a very sharp increase even if these amounts still seem low in comparison with the deutschmark and the dollar which were two to five times more important respectively in 1986.

We should add, too, that two Japanese banks appeared on the list of the world's ten most profitable banks (a position similar to that of the United Kingdom): the Sanwa Bank draws 20 percent of its profits from international operations. Mitsubishi's balance-sheet total in London amounted to over $20 bn at the end of 1986. The Mitsubishi Bank at present has six foreign subsidiaries which account for 15 percent of their profits made outside Japan. Sanwa has four offices in Hong Kong and three representatives in China, and is pursuing its external growth in the United States through acquisitions and repurchases, while diversifying itself geographically.

With the eight large commercial banks firmly established abroad, it is probable that Japan's sixty-four banks[24] will begin a process of internationalization, having been authorized by the Ministry of Finance to open branches and subsidiaries abroad. The largest of these, such as the Hokuriku Bank, do not operate in the same areas as their compatriots who have set up in London. At present, only 2 percent of their income comes from international activities, and foreign assets account for no more than 6 percent of their total assets.

The absolute figures are striking; but what is really important is the sharp rise of these regional banks, and of other types of banks specializing in agricultural credit.

Real Japanese financial power also lies in the hands of the brokers and insurance companies. Japanese commercial banks have a banking strategy which favors their relationship with industry. Sumitomo is driven by a strong expansionist motive. It is determined to acquire world pre-eminence in all aspects of financial activity – as witnessed by its entry into the capital base of Goldman Sachs. These banks often emphasize privileged relationships with medium-sized, dynamic Japanese companies, operating in, among others, the high tech. sector. Sometimes, as in the case of the Norinchukin Bank, their customers include a high proportion of farmers, whose increasingly abundant savings provide these banks with ample captive resources.

Banks no longer have a monopoly on the management of a state's wealth. Insurance companies, which have not yet all set up international investment management structures, are being called on to play an increasingly active role. Of note are the interventions of insurance companies and of British pension funds on the French Treasury bond market, and the involvement of Japanese insurance companies in the United States.

As for the sovereign borrowers with doubtful signatures, it is worth noting that the existence of these debts has a profound impact on the strategy of numerous large banks. The main impact of these debts on the banks' strategy can be summarized as follows.

First of all, the need to set up large provisions has reduced the net cash flow of these institutions and has therefore reduced their score for balance-sheet growth.

Secondly, the existence of high-risk assets means that the banks will be less likely to take other risks, in particular when it comes to financing small and medium-sized companies, international trade or large projects.

Finally, measures to ease the burden of these loans, such as rescheduling, has reduced the banks' liquidity and has led to high costs in managing the balance sheet.

Of course, collaboration between the banks concerned, the export guarantee organizations, the IMF and the World Bank, was stepped up when these countries requested rescheduling of their debts. However, the weakness of some banks resulting from their commitments to certain developing countries can only speed up the process of world concentration of banks and further reduce their ability to allocate resources to the most productive sectors of their national economy, in particular to their local industry.

The corporate market: The big firms and the others

Before looking at the main trends of the corporate market, which consists almost entirely of multinationals, and in order to come to a better understanding of the origin of the exogenous competition in which these companies engage, a distinction must be made between the international and domestic banking arenas. The former involves exogenous competition; the latter, savings banks.[25]

Transnational banking and large firms

The multinational banks have developed a set of operations which display the following features:[26]

1 They do not require a very large number of branches outside the country of origin. Even when exchange controls and means of communication exist, they can be carried out from the head office or from the international financial markets of London, New York, Tokyo, Frankfurt, Zurich, and Paris.
2 Their growth followed the increase of computer networks and intensified after the first oil shock.
3 They are comprised essentially of transactions involving all the closely interconnected markets of Euroassets, foreign currency ($2 trn–$3 trn a day) and futures ($500 bn–$1000 bn a day).

The corporate banking activity remains the most vulnerable to competition, which is exacerbated by the continuing entry of large firms into this market which have the means to implement their strategy. The banks are equipped with expertise, computer systems, telecommunications networks, and equity enabling them to provide the products demanded by the large firms; these firms, themselves well equipped with exchange rooms, systems, networks, and human resources, also have enormous cash reserves. Indeed, it is common for some of the large groups to have liquid assets in excess of their debt (e.g. Nestlé).

The key factors for success in the face of this competitive challenge are the price of the service and the quality of the operators in markets where high quality information and sound judgment on behalf of the bankers affects profitability. This assumes, of course, that these operators will have already found the new products which meet the client's needs. It is therefore necessary for banks to collaborate not only with the big companies but also with brokers, who act as filters between the large firms and the banks and who have a significant role in financial innovation. Indeed, many firms go through brokers to obtain new option products for which the banks also play a role as guarantor between the firms and other counterparts.

On the other hand, they cannot, in the case of commercial

paper issues, bypass the banking system. Indeed, central banks and auditors, at least in France and in the United States, require companies which issue these instruments to have refinancing lines in reserve should access to this market suddenly become uncertain due to, for example, a crisis of confidence. (Union Carbide had to draw on its refinancing lines when faced with the massive withdrawal of its investments after the accident in India.) Such operations earn banks margins which, depending on the state of the market, vary from ⅛ percent to 5 percent. As a result of the implementation of the Cooke Report, these margins will tend to increase.

Despite the economic situation, and in view of their available cash reserves, it is reasonable to believe that the intervention of large firms in the banking business, and in financial activities generally, will continue to grow. We can assume that they will therefore need commercial banks less and less, except as insurers of credit availability or for very specific services or should these institutions develop the human resource capacity and the financial commitment to enter into partnership with their customers in terms of long-range industrial strategy. The organization of the large firms' financial management staffs into autonomous profit-making centers confirms this and leads us to predict a long period of disintermediation where certain firms structurally in the black would lend to those structurally in the red, outside the banking circuit.

One of the necessary conditions for this scenario to become reality, is that the creditor firms set up professionally trained teams to assess and manage credit risk. The limits of such diversification are basically organizational and remain similar to those which at the moment prevent industrial firms which have embarked on consumer credit, such as General Motors, from becoming fully-fledged banks. The industrial organization has its own structures, environment, identity, and culture which condition and impose limits on its strategy.

Hence, industrial firms see their financial diversification possibilities reduced to market slots in which credit risk has almost disappeared or in which the frequency of operations allows a statistical estimate of the risk. Elsewhere, the difficulty of evaluating and controlling risk prevents most industrial firms from encroaching on an area traditionally reserved for banks.

Domestic banking and medium-sized companies

The level of competition here may currently appear lower than in the corporate banking market, but it could intensify sharply in the near future. First of all, these medium-sized firms have the highest growth potential; secondly, they are being increasingly solicited by a growing number of banks, including foreign banks such as Citicorp in the United Kingdom, the Japanese banks in the United Kingdom and California, and the mutual insurance networks in France.

Success here can be summed up principally as the management of a relationship by which an industrial firm perceives a bank as a partner willing to share long-term risks and rewards. Such a partnership is helped by geographical proximity, which not only allows distribution of banking products but is also conducive to a better understanding of the firm's leading personnel and its industrial strategy. The other elements, such as the price or nature of the products, are less important.

In this market subsegment, the leading role played by the Japanese, German, and French banks on their national territory stands in contrast to the more passive attitude of the British and Belgian banks. The chief explanation for this discrepancy is the lack of long-term on-balance-sheet credit in the United Kingdom, the British banks still probably bearing the scars of the banking crisis of the end of the nineteenth century and thereafter handicapped by the absence of internal banking structures devoted to evaluating industrial strategies and assessing the risks linked to them. In Japan and West Germany, on the other hand, the banks benefit from long experience, sometimes over more than a century, in industrial collaboration. Bank departments have been created which specialize in various industries as well as actual equity investment. These relationships mean that a bank will, should the situation so require, continue to support a firm even when the banking margin does not sufficiently remunerate a significant risk. France, with a few exceptions like Suez, Paribas, BNP, and Crédit Lyonnais, is lagging somewhat behind Japan and West Germany in this area and so holds an intermediate position between these countries and the United Kingdom.

Nevertheless, compared with the larger firms, this market remains relatively protected from international competition.[27] Competition has shifted: the geographical origin of the new participants, in terms of international competition, plays only a secondary role to credit supply. Indeed, successful participants are often the ones with the best knowledge of the industrial strategy and technical reliability of their customers. Thus they are in a position to perform arbitrage between industrial prospects and immediate returns, according to terms defined by their general policy.

Individual banking: Estate management and personal financing

The evolution of international financial markets has led banks into new lines of specialization. One of those with a greater potential for development is the management of private wealth. Before studying competition *per se* in this sector, we should look at the logic which led banks to position themselves in this market.

The growth and management of wealth

There are five principal reasons for the growth of financial wealth. First, thirty years of postwar economic growth enabled the accumulation of transnational wealth totalling some $5,000 bn in addition to national liquid wealth. Secondly, for the last few years real interest rates have for the most part been positive. Thirdly, there has been a decline, probably a long-lasting one, in the relative value of numerous non-financial assets, except those characterized by their extreme rarity (works of art, real estate located in the heart of a few large cities). This decline concerns in particular many industrial and agricultural raw materials. There are many reasons for this development in industry. The percentage of raw materials in finished products continues to decrease in value for reasons inherent in present and future industrial processes: the trend toward miniaturization, new technologies (biogenetics will have a tendency to reduce the needs in fertilizers), substitute products, and energy savings. In agriculture, technological progress and its spread to developing countries where manpower can be trained relatively fast (witness for example, Brazil's success in the area of soya beans and wheat) indicates a lasting downward trend in farm commodity prices and therefore in the price of land. It is noteworthy that from 1975 to 1990 the average price of agricultural land in France expressed in constant francs fell 60 percent whereas during this same period the securities index and the price of real estate in Paris rose more than four-fold. And fourthly, the size of the financial market is an important factor which favors this type of investment. Its sophistication, with the emergence of the futures market, enables all the subtleties of risk assumption to be accommodated.

The management of wealth must also take into account the complex international dimension. The investment world has incontrovertibly become international[28] and it requires close monitoring of the evolution of exchange rates and interest-rate differentials. Traditionally based on the possession of a supply of financial assets, investment management today means taking advantage of financial market imbalances.[29] The constant search for the best financial assets on the best markets, or taking advantage of all the opportunities of arbitrage and of position, demands highly professional management of the portfolios mainly entrusted with the large institutions' specialized departments, whose operations must be closely co-ordinated with those of the departments active on the money markets.

The size of the sums at stake gives the bank which specializes in portfolio management a considerable edge, both in terms of cost and in terms of trading capability. The pure brokerage business, without position-taking, can be profitable, since market dynamism means handling of a consistently large number of orders which in turn results in considerable commissions. In the Eurobond market, for example, small and medium-sized orders' brokerage fees (a full circle on $1 m) mean remuneration of the order of $5,000 plus transaction fees which cover the service and expertise provided by the portfolio manager. As for portfolio management costs, they could diminish as competition intensifies, provided that the banks do not have to assume a significant share of the shortfall resulting from portfolio management errors. There are signs that this is becoming increasingly the case.

The movement of international banks toward transferable securities management heightens the competition among them, forcing them to innovate and consequently to widen the gap which separates them from the local banks.

The trend toward internationalization which includes the unification of international financial markets is not complete. There are still differences between the various categories of banks and countries. Not all banks followed the process of transformation which was underway with the same diligence and therefore not all benefited from its effect on the international financial environment. The Japanese, American, and London establishments were in the vanguard of the movement which saw what were small brokerage houses a few years ago (Goldman Sachs, Morgan Stanley, Lazard New York, Paris, and London, and Salomon Brothers, for example) become large global institutions forming relationships with considerable strategic implications, such as Sumitomo's 12.5 percent investment in Goldman Sachs. The same is true for merchant banks, as well as for the new Japanese brokerage houses now participating in the race. Here professionalism in management, creativity, expertise and, primarily, investment and placing capacity and reliable and experienced teams are the competitive advantages.

A global approach to markets and customers has become essential. It will soon be necessary to have an internal knowledge of the different market segments and to introduce for each of them a range of products and a management approach tailored to their requirements.

Personal financing

Personal financing brings into play considerable sums. It represents an important part of the financing of the economy in France, in West Germany, in the United Kingdom and in the United States. The distribution of financing of private individuals among the banks, specialized organizations, and the industrial sector is still fluid, and this sector has become a priority objective of industrialists, of the distribution sector, and of banks and insurance companies.

Specialized organizations such as Citicorp in the USA and worldwide, Compagnie Bancaire in France, the KundenKreditbank in West Germany (a Citicorp subsidiary), and hire-purchase companies in Japan and the United Kingdom have their own sales and marketing network along with specialized and powerful computer equipment. They use debt-collecting methods, particularly in Japan, which banks have hitherto been loth to adopt, including tactics which range from approaching employers to (sometimes) even harassment and physical pressure.

The market of financial organizations: A look at the activity of competing banks

Interbank competition is alluded to throughout this book. Here it will suffice to identify the salient points likely to condition its evolution.[30]

Two major considerations characterize this sector. On the one hand, it is here more than elsewhere that information technology comes most strongly into play. Indeed, it is necessary to ensure that large amounts of capital can be moved under optimal conditions of cost, security, and information. The management of these flows will create new opportunities for the bank, which could make its technological tool also available to large industrial firms, all of which need it to manage considerable flows of cash and information. And the position of banks will be further reinforced by the creation of privileged links through the control of funds movement.

Nevertheless, in so far as management of these funds includes a set of risks that are hard to quantify, the large clearing banks suddenly find themselves confronted with a problem of risk management somewhat comparable to that of a central bank. Indeed, at any moment these flows created through exchange operations or deposits,[31] or on futures markets, can be either misappropriated or poorly allocated, representing cumulative amounts lacking any relation to the financial standing of counterparts. It was in an effort to limit this risk that the Federal Reserve issued in 1987 precise rules concerning maximum overdraft amounts for a given period within one day, or from one day to the next. The same approach is being adopted by the Bank of England and other European and Asian central banks.

World funds transfer networks are mainly structured so that only a few banks can communicate among themselves in real time, thus ensuring from an international point of view the function of world clearing banks. At present, these banks are increasingly forced by the central banks to limit their global risk per institution and to back up this activity with very large amounts of equity.

Such an evolution could eventually result in a change in the method of remunerating this activity,[32] to include the costs linked to the mobilization of equity rather than just the depreciation of computer and electronic physical capital.

3

◇

The Regulatory Constraint

◆

The performances of banking organizations and other financial institutions are conditioned by the regulations imposed by the supervisory bodies. These diverse bodies themselves come under the direction of the public authorities and can give multiple forms to public intervention.

REGULATION: THE BACKGROUND[1]

The objectives of the monetary authorities: The logic of regulation/deregulation

Intervention by the public monetary authorities in the banking sector has two main objectives: preserving the security of the banking system and reinforcing the efficiency of financial markets. Recent changes in banking, with the creation of new products and technological developments, have had significant impact on these two objectives.

Reinforcing the security of the financial system

Preservation of the integrity of the financial system was the principal aim of so-called microeconomic supervision. The problems posed by this form of supervision have increased with the transformations and upheavals which have occurred on the markets and the upsurge of financial intermediaries.[2]

Two imperatives, often contradictory, limit the area in which today's monetary authorities can intervene: it is necessary, on the one hand, to adhere strictly to the usual rules of caution and, on the other hand, to maintain the flexibility necessary for the financial system to adapt in an ever riskier environment.

The general principles governing this form of supervision are formulated by identifying:

- the kind of financial intermediaries that should be subject to control: which institutions must be monitored?
- the area over which this control must be exercised: all or part of an institution's operations?
- the degree of homogeneity of the forms of control, considering the diversity of the institution in question. In other words, must similar standards of control be applied to institutions exercising different activities?

The trend is toward a gradual increase in the number of institutions subject to control. The need for such an extensive definition has also led the authorities to adopt the principle of control on the basis of consolidated accounts. This principle is justified on at least two fundamental counts. First, such a viewpoint reflects the behavior of operators in financial markets, who make their evaluations on the basis of a global perspective which includes the financial situation of the parent company, of the subsidiaries, even of the branch offices engaged in non-banking activities. This mirrors the advent of banking strategies which call for a global approach to the management of assets and liabilities. Secondly, this option tackles evasions and other techniques for getting around domestic regulations, by extending control to all establishments linked to the parent company, whether resident or not. This recourse to supervision based on the principle of consolidation still leaves room for control on a non-consolidated basis: an assessment can be made from each institution's balance sheet, from its cash reserves, and/or from its off-balance-sheet commitments. However, numerous problems arise because of disparities in the structures of the various institutions. There are also practical difficulties concerning the disparate nature of monitoring techniques, of norms imposed on banks, of differences in monitoring objectives, and of the relative weight attached to the efficiency of markets, of competition, and of monetary policy. These difficulties will, however, diminish as legal barriers between the various competitive institutions are lifted.

Whatever the pace of these developments, difficult choices are in store for the monitoring authorities, who will have to decide on the range of permitted activities of financial institutions and on the degree of access to banking operations that fundamentally non-financial institutions should be allowed. In time, these institutions will have to be monitored: the allocation of credit to the public implies fiduciary responsibility and a guarantee of good management which requires the supervisory authorities to ensure that business is conducted in accordance with professional standards, and with the ethical obligations of the profession of banker, manager, and guarantor of public savings. However, in several countries, the restrictions placed on banking have been gradually removed, a trend linked to a philosophy of intervention which seeks to favor the financial innovation process while reinforcing market discipline and limiting the possible appearance of new risks.

As new instruments and new techniques appear, the methods used to monitor risks are continuously being refined. The development of new technical procedures, such as electronic payments, make the system more vulnerable; the difficulty of ensuring that the computer installations and the concentrated information in the databases are safe considerably increases operating risks.

Three principal areas appear to have dictated the attitude adopted by the monetary authorities on this subject. First of all, they strive to use the new monitoring techniques offered by statistical data processing for the identification and evaluation of risk. Secondly, their action is marked by their interest in developing a dynamic system of control which can be adapted to the environment. Thirdly, they seek to control the risks born of new types of operations and products.

Recent experience with risk evaluation has shown considerable progress, in particular for foreign exchange risk, industry and company risk, statistical risk, country risk, transformation risk, and finally, risks arising from the strategy of a bank in terms of human and/or technological resources or choice of market segment.

The way in which these controls are exercised varies from country to country. In the United Kingdom it is extremely discreet. Most control there consists of thorough and probing meetings with executive directors where the principal orientations of their establishments are discussed, on the basis of budget, strategy and summary accounting documents. The Bank of England does not yet have an inspection body comparable to that of the Federal Reserve Bank or the Bank of France. The West German approach consists of formulating global directives and leaving risk assessment and strategy to the bankers, ensuring only the application of the controls laid down and compliance with pre-defined risk limitation standards.

However, the new element in the area of microeconomic supervision is the complexity of control arising from the emergence of new risks linked to the development of data processing, new products, and the large degree of financial markets' volatility. Assessing and measuring these risks precisely has not yet been possible because deregulation is relatively recent, because financial markets are increasingly international, and because most new products have a brief life cycle.

The difficulty of evaluating at their fair value traditional market-related risks also affects operations involving swaps, on-lending, and even certain interbank operations. Furthermore, the accumulation of off-balance-sheet commitments has become a subject of concern for the authorities, who believe that these items must be reintegrated in the calculation of equity ratios.

The developments described in chapter 1 have also led the authorities to adopt a system of surveillance based on cash flows. However, these flows have been largely influenced by new management techniques and the authorities have found themselves faced with the difficulty of assessing the degree of liquidity and the exact maturity date for all the components of a bank's assets/liabilities mix, as well as seeking criteria by which in practice they can measure the bank's ability to procure liquid funds on the money market.

Despite these difficulties, the trend currently adopted by the regulatory authorities is toward orientating the control of liquidity around two principles. On the one hand, attention is focused on the current and potential structure of bank financing. The banks have been encouraged to increase their own financial resources and to improve their ability to mobilize equity funds. On the other hand, greater importance is given to the failure to match maturity dates than to the bank's liquidity and cash flows. Also, the authorities perceive that a more elaborate differentiation of the control techniques of asset/liabilities management is needed, and greater attention should be paid to the level of bank equity in relation to the nature of the risks assumed.

The need to reinforce levels of equity and provisions has become one of the major concerns of supervisors. Certainly, sufficient equity nurtures confidence and protects against possible losses. It must be noted, however, that the bank's profit-earning capacity and latent reserves, often comprised of undervalued assets, represent the first lines of defense against events which would require sizeable provisions. Once again, the proliferation of new participants with complex economic characteristics leads to problems of measurement and definition. Defining comparable standards of equity for banks which have various ways of building up reserves, of accounting, of assessing assets and liabilities is difficult. The search for unified standards is a major theme of debate between monetary authorities. At present, efforts are being made to reach an agreement on certain definitions, which now rest on objective criteria. Here too the question arises of off-balance-sheet liabilities, which until recently, have not been fully covered by equity.

In the event, it has finally been acknowledged that it is up to the bank's management, in agreement with the auditors (who are becoming more vigilant in the United States and United Kingdom), to determine the level of reserves to be retained. The role of the authorities is to ensure that the banks prepare a conservative and realistic evaluation of their assets. The difficulty of assessing risks is also due to the fact that there is no uncontested standard of assessment of certain risks – country and credit risks, for example; it follows, therefore, that the qualitative dimension remains essential and the supervisory bodies will accordingly focus on judging the experience of management.

Parallel to verification by supervisors and other monetary authorities runs the question of reinforcement of the stability and security of the financial system through market-imposed discipline. Market discipline rests on three major elements:

1 the ability of market participants to detect and to react to changes in risk;
2 the capacity of the institution's executives to react rapidly and effectively to market signals;
3 the authorities' reaction to any serious difficulties encountered by the institutions.

Opinion today tends to the view that a better understanding of the need for self-discipline on the part of all market players does not mean that the authorities have no role. Since the conditions for perfect market discipline, e.g. access to detailed information on the situation of banks and of other intervening parties, are rarely fulfilled, market discipline has fairly obvious limits.

Within the framework of this accepted discipline, there is no disagreement on the distribution of responsibilities between bank management and the controlling authorities. The former bear responsibility for the bank's security and soundness through day-to-day management and the implementation of a long-term strategic plan; the latter must ensure that the inspectors and systems of control are in place within each bank, and that they comply with the required norms and criteria.

One of the questions which has not been addressed in sufficient depth concerns the role of central banks as a lender of last resort and the intervention measures which would be taken in case of major crisis. The investment of $6 bn by the FDIC and the Federal Reserve Bank in the failing Continental Illinois bank testifies to the validity of this question.

Deregulation

The areas subject to regulation have changed over time and in space, to take into account the historical and cultural particularities, the importance assigned to financial institutions in the economy, and finally legislation. Limitations have successively been placed on growth, in order to discourage unwise decisions; on oligopolistic practices, in order not to harm the efficiency of the financial system; and finally, on conditions for entering and exiting the banking sector.

Recent technical changes and changes in attitude of the main players in world financial markets have led the authorities to adopt a further policy on regulation: to adjust the regulatory structure in order to better reinforce bank security and to improve the contribution of these institutions to economic priorities. There again the authorities must reconcile the two contrasting imperatives, a desirable degree of competition and the need to maintain a stable and sound financial system.

The trend toward interest-rate deregulation has been one area where this policy has been applied in an attempt to make markets more efficient. The factors which enabled this deregulation to continue are various: the large scale of disintermediation, the appearance at a sustained pace of new markets and instruments, the structural transformation of customer behavior, the intensification and generalization of competitive factors on a global level, and finally, the possibilities offered by new funds transfer technologies.

This process of deregulation is not yet complete; some countries, such as Portugal, Spain, and Italy, still have entire sectors where the determination of interest rates does not obey market logic, leading therefore to special rates. Nevertheless, deregulation is bringing about changes in the relationship between free interest rates and special rates, making management of these circuits more complex and leaving room for unpredictable distortions in the movement of financial flows. Also, the authorities have preferred to introduce deregulation on a step-by-step basis, introducing it successively in selected areas. The possibility of extending deregulation to the benefit of other bank activities depends on the efficiency of the markets, the security of the financial system, and that system's oligopolistic structure.

It is undeniable that the fiercer competition among banks needs to be tempered by strict and better targeted surveillance, and this demands rapid detection of undesirable practices by certain banks which may let the structure of their balance sheets deteriorate or lead them to take excessive risks.

The authorities, then, must come up with a regulatory arsenal which favors conditions for creating and exercising new activities at a level of risk considered tolerable for the community. When competition reaches a certain degree of intensity, the banks can move into new arenas of more profitable activity to offset the decrease in their profit margins. Innovation, however, can be taken to the point where the risks incurred become excessive. These risks are exacerbated by the hostile reaction of firms already established in the sector, to which less experienced new entrants will inevitably be vulnerable. Consequently, the authorities are moving toward a more selective approach in granting rights to engage in new activities, simultaneously evaluating, case by case, the additional contribution to the efficiency of markets and to economic development that these activities can make.

In spite of such caution, there is a fear that deregulation will result in greater concentration in the banking and financial system. One might think that such a move toward concentration would in the long term work against the interests of consumers of banking services. However, the recent emergence of the so-called contestable markets theory and practice shows that firms in limited numbers can behave efficiently. All that needs to be done is to maintain the beneficial pressure of potential entrants in the market.

In this respect, the general tendency to dismantle regulatory obstacles to the foreign banks' entry into domestic markets can be welcomed as a positive development. Adhering to its traditions, banking has not only stood out as a sector where there has not been a resurgence of protectionism but, better still, it is one of the few sectors open to the liberalization of its operations on a world scale. In so far as deregulation eliminates certain artificial obstacles in the way of banking operations, non-bank establishments might feel less encouraged to enter these areas of activity, even if they retain a competitive edge in other areas. They could, of course, take advantage of the possibilities offered by technology and progress in information processing to use payment mechanisms and intermediation functions; however, the monetary authorities are likely to adopt a cautious attitude toward the widespread entry of non-bank establishments in the banking business, for this development would render problematic a good definition of currency and pose difficulties in the control of banks, especially in countries where banking is narrowly defined.

In these conditions, the evolution of banking structures toward a system of equality with other institutions in possible areas of shared activity must be considered a long-term and uncertain process.

The inequality of treatment stemming from conditions of competition remains acute in systems where private and state-funded public institutions subject to the same regulatory constraints coexist. This inequality will be reduced over time, since the public institutions will be subject to management principles similar to those of private sector banks. Even so, institutions which can benefit from the state's guarantee and therefore undertake operations with less equity than their private sector counterparts need will have an advantage in that respect. Moreover, institutional constraints and large public deficits can prevent governments from increasing the capital of the banks they own as they should (as, for example, Italy, France, and Belgium). These factors render reinforcement of the public banks' shareholder equity with regard to their private competitors even less likely.

Regulation and banking strategy

Deregulation being a recent phenomenon, it is impossible to identify all its consequences for banks' strategy. However, the lifting of certain constraints has already had numerous repercussions,[3] such as:

- an increase in banks' liability costs;
- greater competition between all the participating players in the financial areas;
- a change in the composition of the banks' profit and loss.

The increase in the percentage of banks' and non-bank financial institutions' liabilities which bear interest at the market rate has increased the cost of collecting deposits and will have at least the following consequences:

- increased automation in order to reduce costs and, especially, to create new products;
- increased and better targeted prices for services, an inevitable consequence of decreased margins;
- the development of loans at variable rates according to the degree of risk, which reduces the propensity to take significant and long-term risks in managing the assets/liabilities mix;
- longer lending periods, in particular to further promote the development of "securitization" which enables long-term loans to be placed with institutional investors, or even with individuals.

This trend leads financial institutions to transfer some of the credit and interest rate risks to individual and institutional investors who, thanks to deregulation, saw the potential for greater return on their savings increased, which in turn enabled them to assume greater risks.

The enrichment of the financial sector by technological innovations will mean that only about thirty banks of world status will have the necessary resources to develop and to implement the very specialized systems adapted to each market segment and to each large geographical region.

Despecialization, that is to say, enlarging the banking system's definition of its business activity, will increase the number of key factors for customer success. The originality and performance of insurance and cash products, the range of services offered, and the capacity to communicate the added value of these services will, in the future, help determine the ability of banks to take and keep market share.

Finally, the increased rates offered on retail deposits place organizations which finance themselves in the market on a near-equal footing with those which manage a large resource-gathering network. The existence of a branch network remains, however, a major asset, provided that over the years its establishment has followed the demographic changes and the new consumer expectations.

Nevertheless, deregulation does not offer the same opportunities to all financial institutions. Once again we must distinguish between global and regional banks. The former see less inconvenience in the elimination of regulated deposit returns: they are traditionally less dependent on captive deposits because they procure funds largely by issuing certificates of deposit ("CDs") or on the money market.

Regional banks, however, depend heavily on captive deposits. Having set up branch networks for the collection of savings, they are now beset by the increased yields on savings and by the probable decline of their geographical monopoly. These banks will be the first victims of today's deregulation, unless they apply rigorous industrial methods to the management of their business.

For the savings banks the consequences of deregulation are mixed, to say the least. They see the scope of their activity widened, but on the other hand face the loss of the advantages which set them apart from the network of commercial banks. They can issue credit cards, install automatic tellers, offer cash management, invest in corporate and other bonds, and, of course, pursue their traditional activity of offering mortgages. The best strategy will be that which enables them to offset lower margins by being selective and providing high-quality services at an attractive return. In the absence of such a strategy, they remain penalized by the considerable increase in the cost of their resources and of managing their network.

Globally, deregulation will lead to a displacement of customers, to a degree which will vary from country to country and bank to bank, indicating an end to monopolies yielding significant profits. The banks will react to this by accelerating the process of change of their cost structure, which essentially comprises of personnel costs. This is a critical issue: a bank's major investment is in its employees. Personnel costs should therefore be considered as long-term investments, and the process of adaptation should consist in gradually modifying the composition of employee expenses by eliminating those which relate to repetitive tasks and by investing in people highly specialized in the areas of information technology, marketing, and consulting, in particular, in corporate strategy.

In addition, the development of variable interest rates, allowing more direct transmission of monetary policy signals, could create a new way of indexing the economy, thus reinforcing the role of monetary policy, especially since the structure of the yield on savings encourages households to have a strong preference for liquidity, which results in an upsurge in low-risk investments.[4]

In short, the effects of deregulation, acting on the principal markets, can be summed up as follows:

- increased cost of collecting deposits;
- lower profitability of the traditional banking activities;
- higher costs for financial services;
- acceleration of world technological innovation;
- tendency toward a strong concentration of the financial system;
- better yield on savings to the benefit of creditors, and to the detriment of debtors;
- shifting of debt and interest rate risk to individual and institutional investors through securitization;
- increased sensitivity of the economy to monetary policy by way of interest rates;
- greater complexity of the world financial system;
- inevitably, the eventual emergence of new forms of controls, either exogenous by the central banks, or endogenous through a stronger pre-eminence of the auditing function which will have to encompass all the methods of reducing credit, market, and operational risks;

- awareness by senior management of the essential importance, in such a changing context, of control and strategy functions.

DEREGULATION OF THE AMERICAN ECONOMY

The evolution of the US regulatory system has been vitally important because it has to an extent spread to the rest of the world.

Deregulation in the USA became necessary because of the inadequacy of the rules and regulations in force, whose main objective was to preserve the security of the banking system as it then operated. This security is expressed for the most part in terms of:

1 available liquid assets: the abundancy of securities in the market of all maturities and in all the main currencies, combined with the ability to buy/sell assets thanks to securitization, has considerably reduced the risk of liquidity crisis;
2 quality of assets: the banks no longer have a monopoly over knowledge of debtors' risks; this information is for the most part more widely accessible, whether it concerns assessment of the statistical risk for individuals, or the credit risk, which is reliably evaluated by specialized organizations such as Standard and Poor and Moody for multinational firms, and by international organizations for countries.

Deregulation is justified by the changes it produces in real added value for the different players in the financial markets:

- reduction of the placing and analytical capacity of brokers, to the benefit of institutional investors;
- reduction of the banks' monopoly over risk analysis for individuals and for some small and medium-sized companies, to the benefit of distribution networks and industrial suppliers;
- dilution of the banks' monopoly on wholesale liquid funds, since many multinational companies have large reserves of cash;

- reduction of privileged access by banks to financial information, with access to networks like Reuters now common;
- new consumer requirements of financial products in terms of simplified access and diversification.

All these market transformations have invalidated a large number of regulations and therefore brought about deregulation.

The American banks have to meet four challenges. They must:

1. make considerable investments in Asia and in Europe in order to protect their position as banks of world status. No American bank, except for Citicorp, and then only in part, has the resources in people and in capital to play a significant role in these two regions. Since 1975, the international strategies of most other American banks, with the exception of Morgan Guaranty and Bankers Trust, have been a relative failure (in particular those of the Bank of America and the Chase Manhattan Bank);
2. make large provisions to cover doubtful industrial and commercial debts, in particular in the United States (where prices of agricultural products and real estate and leveraged buy-outs have turned sour) and abroad (relating especially to maritime affreightment, oil explorations and real estate and leisure developments);
3. face the transformation of information technology which calls into play considerable sums and significant risks, especially when a multisector and global approach is adopted;
4. cope with the deterioration of the quality of credits granted to developing countries, with the resulting decrease in liquidity, large potential losses, and a decline in share price.

The influence of the world context on the financial situation of American banks is illustrated by what has happened to the yields of certain types of assets, notably land and real estate assets, heavily penalized by the situation of the world economy. Furthermore, American farmers, some of whom had gone into debt to finance an expansion of export crops and were caught off guard by the change in the economic situation, found themselves unable to reimburse the mortgages that they had taken out by selling land, and many farm-lending institutions consequently are going bankrupt. These risks of bankruptcy may lead to reinforced government control in this area, whose complex organizational structure is already marked by a strong state presence. Indeed, the "Farm Credit System" created in 1916 by the US Federal Government holds 37 percent of the private farm debt and eleven of its thirty-seven constituent banks have doubtful debts exceeding their capital. In addition to the private network made up by the regional commercial banks, there exists the "Farmer Home Administration" which holds 15 percent of the farm debt and presides over a network of twelve regional farmers' banks on which three farming credit organizations depend: a mortgage bank, a production financing short-term loan bank, and a local bank for co-operative farms.

The difficulties felt by the agricultural sector are mirrored in the real estate and energy sectors, where similar restructuring can be expected.

The measures taken by the Federal authorities consist in enlarging the guarantee granted by the Federal Deposit Insurance Company (FDIC) for deposits under or equal to $100,000 to include all deposits. The FDIC also assumed $4.5 bn worth of doubtful debts, making itself a majority shareholder in Continental Illinois, and a consortium of twenty-eight banks set up a credit line of $5.5 bn.

Comparable difficulties have been encountered by the Savings and Loan Associations which have absorbed over $180 bn in junk bonds,[5] whose payment is far from assured in economic circumstances of prolonged recession. Cumulative losses in that sector could reach a staggering $300 bn.

Must this always be thought about but never discussed?

At present, supervision of the bank system is based on two proposals by the directors of the Federal Reserve System. One consists in increasing the ratio of equity to total capital from 6 percent to 9 percent, the other in reinforcing the banking deposit insurance system, this reinforcement to be in the form of adjustment of the insurance premium according to risks taken by the bank and particularly risks taken abroad.

Gradual deregulation of the financial system is thus accompanied by a reinforcement of central bank control, which increases insurance requirements along with the rise in risks.

The consequences for the financial system of these trends, which are more complementary than contradictory, will be threefold:[6]

1 modernization of the banking system, made possible by the banks' desire to control their costs in the face of greater competition and to improve their margins by means of new products and services;
2 concentration, favored by a changing environment in which the policy of deregulation continues;
3 harmonization of banking regulations, resulting from despecialization and the gradual challenging of the Glass–Steagall Act.

THE WORLD ASPECTS OF DEREGULATION

The spread of deregulation from the United States has come about in various ways, having reached countries with widely differing banking systems.

Deregulation only occurs when the risks which justified regulation diminish, but risks hitherto unknown, such as market risks and operating risks, can also emerge and form the basis of new legislation. This explains the current lull before new difficulties, perceived or anticipated, give rise to a package of restrictive measures. The facts often impose themselves before people have perceived the need. It is clear that we are in a period of transition preceding changes which the public authorities are already intuitively sensing, with the recognition of new risks underscored by the Bank for International Settlements.[7]

National deregulation programs

Because a country's maturity in terms of deregulation is closely dependent on the collective aversion to risk, it is hardly surprising that experiences differ from one country to the next. The United Kingdom, for example, remains most strongly committed to deregulation,[8] whereas Japan resists it most; France and West Germany stand between these two positions, although there is more deregulation in France than in Germany or Belgium.

The United Kingdom

Deregulation in the United Kingdom began with the removal of all restrictions on deposits. Banks were authorized to pay interest on day-to-day savings, to set the rate on fixed deposits, to free themselves from exchange controls. Commercial banks were permitted to take control of merchant banks. Then we saw the gradual integration of all the functions of stockbrokers, prompting the almost total disappearance of independent intermediation.

Just as new was the attitude of the Bank of England which, after defending for several decades the principle of separation and autonomy of management between merchant banks and commercial banks, now accepts that the takeover of merchant banks may be accompanied by a process of integration. Such a change resulted in authority being transferred to those with the mass of capital; which in the United Kingdom, meant the clearing banks. Hence we witnessed a series of mergers. NatWest, Barclays, and Midland began by acquiring an investment in merchant banks with which they had maintained for a long time a relationship of underwriter; then the banks were gradually integrated and their exchange rooms and their data-processing centers pooled. However, success in this depends on holding back from total integration, because each body, to maintain its efficiency in its area, must see its specific culture protected, anchored in a particular form of human resource management.

British deregulation had a number of victims among the brokers, commercial banks, and merchant banks.

Considering the equity required to be a credible counterpart, there are very few British merchant banks able to remain independent. Only Warburg and Lazard Brothers appear capable of this feat, on the basis of a strong culture and tradition, outstanding teams, and, in the former case, sizeable industrial and financial holdings built up over several decades.

The large insurance companies and pension funds will play an essential role in the immediate future. These institutions have considerable resources: the forty largest insurance companies and pension funds manage over £250 bn. Because the British insurance system is a capitalization system, not a distribution system, their funds grow particularly rapidly. At the moment they are concerned with modernizing their network and their management methods, but the expansion of the range of their interventions in the financial area in the near future cannot be ruled out.

The competition born of deregulation is not limited to British financial institutions. There is foreign competition from firms such as Citicorp and Compagnie Bancaire who are looking to develop an automated network or to enter consumer banking.

Deregulation in Great Britain has seen a large influx of foreign banks into London, although the host sectors, the Euromarket and capital markets, are different from the traditional markets.[9] Japanese banks, generally absent from the consumer credit sector, captured significant market share in other sectors thanks to a policy of aggressive pricing, to the strength of their domestic economy and to the quality of their UK management, capable of mobilizing group resources.

Japanese strategy: Two recent examples

The logic of the Japanese strategy is evident in four areas: banking, direct investment in securities and real estate and management of longer-maturity securities, pension funds and investment management, and mergers and acquisitions.

The brokerage activities Before looking at the development of brokerage activities, two striking points are worth mentioning:

1 the size of large Japanese brokerage firms in terms of stock exchange capitalization and of net profits in comparison with their counterparts in the United States and the United Kingdom;
2 the consequences of size on their method of intervention, in their ability to subscribe the entirety of a very large bond or stock issue, and to diversify toward banking in London, where Nomura and Daiwa have achieved bank status.

Competition from these firms in banking could have considerable repercussions because they have so many decisive natural competitive advantages:

- access to advanced information technology;
- intimate knowledge of market activities;
- access to privileged knowledge of the industrial strategies of Japanese groups located in the sectors of the future, with the beneficial consequences in terms of lending activities;
- immediate capacity to manage cash;
- absence of operating costs linked to outdated banking structures (branch networks with their cumbersome central services);
- a reservoir of people with a thorough knowledge of the American, British, and German financial (and, to a lesser degree, industrial) fabric.

The Group of Thirty study on brokerage activities mentioned above emphasized the growth of this sector. Japanese legislation maintains a separation between banking and brokerage activities and the debate on Japan's role in international brokerage activities tends to be limited to discussion of what roles to assign brokerage firms. The profit from these firms comes to a large extent from the enormous volume of transactions on the Tokyo Stock Exchange, the largest in the world in 1989 before that of New York, in terms of both the volume of transactions and stock exchange capitalization. Moreover, even if the eighty-three firms on the Tokyo Stock Exchange do not make a very large membership compared with the 600 on the New York Stock Exchange, it must be noted that a limited number of foreign firms have been authorized to become members.

Also notable is trading in government bonds, which rose in monthly volume from ¥3.7 trn in October 1983 to ¥93 trn in October 1984 – an annual growth rate of $4,400 bn. Turnover in private and public bonds quadrupled in four years; even if the current amount appears small in comparison with the size of the American market, once again, attention must be focused on growth.

This large local base has placed Japanese brokerage firms among the most profitable in the world and their placing power has made them fearsome competitors.

Although the large American firms tend to dominate the Eurobond market, Nomura Securities doubled in volume and the value of its issues moved it from fifteenth to tenth position in 1984. In 1990 it will probably be number one. In 1984, the Japanese houses listed among the thirty most important players in the Eurobond market saw their combined share of the market increase, whereas the German banks witnessed a decrease – a problem to which we will return in part II. The same phenomenon can be observed six years later.

Japanese competition in this area is not limited to brokerage firms. Indeed, the prohibition resulting from the regulatory separation between banks and brokerage firms only applies to domestic business. Long-term credit banks see internationalization as an opportunity to resume their normal activities, from which they find themselves excluded by domestic legislation. The London Japanese banks are therefore delighted to meet the challenge from the dominant brokerage firms outside Japan, thereby proving their ability in this area and earning their reintroduction on local Japanese markets, sometime in the future.

Pension funds and management of other investments Estimates of the value of private pension funds in Japan are controversial. Nevertheless, we can evaluate the amount at approximately $500 m in 1968, $55 bn in 1982 and probably $100 bn in 1990.

To this could be added $200 bn in public pension funds currently reinvested in public assets. The management of these funds belongs solely to the trust banks and insurance companies. Prospects of profit in this area seem small: nevertheless, there are certain opportunities for direct acquisition for foreigners, the most plausible alternative being investment consulting.

Indeed, the most interesting option for a foreign institution is probably the provision of consulting services to insurance companies and pension funds in the area of foreign investment. The proportion of foreign securities held by these companies had risen rapidly even before deregulation in 1980. In 1975, foreign securities accounted for no more than 0.5 percent of securities held. This percentage rose from 8.5 percent in 1980 to 22.5 percent in 1983: $12 bn, representing approximately 8 percent of total assets. The financial authorities limit the maximum amount of securities invested abroad to around 10 percent. Even if many institutions rapidly reach this ceiling, the amounts still available in absolute terms are considerable and are bound to rise. To this must be added the additional funds of trust banks whose foreign resources rose from $600 m in March 1982 to $2.5 bn in 1984, a little over 7 percent of their total assets.

This growth in foreign assets was accompanied by a rapid growth in foreign branch offices of insurance companies and pension funds. Insurance companies have, at present, just twenty-eight representative offices and sixteen subsidiaries abroad, whereas pension funds have a considerable foreign network. Statistics published in 1984 reveal that net acquisitions of foreign securities by Japanese investors amounted to $58 bn, of which two-thirds were allocated to brokerage firms on the order of other investors. Over one-fifth of the total, however, went to insurance companies and pension funds whose global investment amounted to $11 bn. By far the most sizeable share of these resources was invested in government bonds, mainly in North America and Australia. A relatively small percentage ($1.5 bn) was devoted to the purchase of shares which was virtually offset by previous sales.

It is possible to predict that the large amount of funds

available for investment will modify the strategy of Japanese banks by encouraging them:

- to make their foreign investment strategies more systematic;
- to include a larger number of securities in their portfolios;
- to diversify their investments geographically.

The international strategies of Japanese firms are illustrated by the examples of firms such as Nippon Life Insurance which, in January 1985, created a London subsidiary specializing in investment operations, following on from those opened the previous year in Luxemburg, Panama, and the United States. Similarly Chiyoda Life established a fully-owned subsidiary in Luxemburg on the same day that Nippon opened its London office.

The trend is toward the creation by the insurance companies of similar subsidiaries: Yasuda in Hong Kong, for instance, and Dowa in Luxemburg. Among these numerous examples, the establishment of Mitsubishi in London in January 1985 was one of the most spectacular. The avowed objective of Mitsubishi Finance Corporation (MFC) is to become a merchant bank, drawing on the experience of the Mitsubishi Corporation as an increasingly diversified industrial and financial group.

Banks in competition with industry

In addition to the competition between financial institutions, illustrated here by the Japanese example, there is, as we have already seen, competition between the banks and industry. Some of the strategies which account for the emergence of this competition were discussed earlier. The changes in cost structures brought about by technological progress have enabled some industrial firms to equip themselves with a sophisticated telecommunications infrastructure. General Motors, for example, has a telecommunications network, the power of which is comparable to that of the largest international banks (Citicorp apart). The entry of numerous industrial manufacturers into the financial world was followed by that of distributors; the existence of a point of sale or a range of products has enabled these firms to familiarize themselves with not only the product that they offer, but the habits, the motivations, and the behavior of their existing or potential customers. Also, after identifying the customers' needs, they are able to control the financing of their product and from there to enlarge the range of financial products offered.

Finally, it must also be noted that the success of these firms owes much to the price of their service. The cost of credit is often less expensive than in banks. In the 1960s and 1970s, quality borrowers discovered that they could obtain money at a lower rate than that being charged by the banks. Between the periodic deadlines for tax payments and the maturity dates of their debts, the firms had considerable quantities of liquid funds that they tied up for weeks. The banks found a way to tap these funds by issuing certificates of deposit, but they had to lend them on at a rate sufficiently profitable to enable them to cover both management costs and risks of default. However, these services could also be provided by a growing number of securities trading firms or even brokerages with very low overheads. They could serve as intermediaries between borrowers and investors at a lower cost, allowing many borrowers to pay less interest on loans and give investors better returns. In the 1970s top credit rated companies issued their own securities to other companies which were in opposite phases of their cash cycle thus circumventing banks. In 1982, the quantity of commercial paper on the market reached four-fifths of the total outstanding of commercial and industrial credit intended for the American banking system![10]

In the light of this development it is possible to predict, in so far as credit-dominated financial products continue to be sought by non-bank enterprises, that only those companies predominantly involved in estate management will continue to represent a relatively captive market for banks for any length of time.

Consumer credit can effectively be securitized and distributed by many large industrial firms which have a captive consumer market and advanced information technology, provided that they evaluate the risk on the basis of statistical standards made available by the existence of a representative sample and that they ensure refinancing, which is facilitated by the liquidity of national and international financial markets. The temptations to do this are enhanced by accounting rules which enable them to consolidate their group accounts without including their financial activities in the balance sheet.

The ideal place for this competition is of course the United States where the quality of available information facilitates entry into the sector. Thus, if a firm like General Motors can today begin to develop the skills needed to expand in the consumer credit sector, nothing can prevent it from continuing its metamorphosis later by expanding its financial activity to include the management of funds for the general public. Limits in this area will mainly be regulatory. However, the existence of current regulatory obstacles does not mean that the other activities are protected. The case of cash management, where the banks are attacked from all sides, is quite enlightening. Here, there is no limit to competition. It is possible simply to set up a financial consultancy firm, itself linked to a broker or a bank which is acquainted with a few well-off investors, and, over time, to offer them the required quality of services.

In the face of this steeply rising competition, the banks can choose from several strategies, which together fall into two groups: the defensive and the offensive.[11] A bank's first reaction would be to consider an alliance with its competitors in identical industrial sectors in order to capture as many financial flows as possible. The banks can also, through a network of minitels and automatic tellers, try to reach a much larger population. That, at least, is the lesson to be learned from the failure of certain banks which had difficulty in properly targeting their customers. Teller networks must reach a maximum number of individuals and at the same time be oriented toward segments that are sufficiently well targeted for changes in habits and sociological behavior not to make the networks obsolete. Once this is achieved, the banks will be able to distribute credits and manage the new product efficiently in the market slots that they occupy, as illustrated by the Citicorp approach.

Within the banks themselves, the decisive factor which will

allow a bank to increase its market share will be its proximity to its customers. This contention may seem paradoxical, given that the widespread use of the minitel will immediately annul the distance gap. Nevertheless, the slow rate of adoption of minitels in the personal finance niche at present justifies the assertion. Over 75 percent of those with significant personal wealth are between 45 and 75 years of age and are often hesitant to turn to minitels, being used to personal relationships of trust between banker and customer. It may take ten to twenty years (especially in Europe) before changes in habits and behavior reach the point where home terminals can be used profitably.

Finally, no discussion of banking competition in the individual sector is complete without mention of the competitive pressure which will be exerted by the insurance companies. The financial power of these institutions which have simultaneously the distribution network for individuals, the necessary management methods, and a wealth of privileged information on customers, makes them significant potential rivals for the near future.

The diversity of systems: Changing balances

Rebalancing the banking sector is a local process for, once again, the banks' competition for individuals is partly frozen by the existing counter system: in this area, market share changes gradually. Customer movement within or between banks is slow to the point where one of the main factors behind a customer's choice of bank is still geographical proximity.

In Japan, moreover, there still exist considerable tax benefits for the savings collected by the banks at favorable rates, although these privileges have been, and will continue to be, considerably eroded. The financial authorities have not, at present, authorized the banks to invest in brokers. Finally, the distinction between commercial bank and merchant bank is contrary to Japanese tradition, since the banks and industrial groups have always shared similar interests with the declared and almost exclusive aim of fostering industry and its growth on a world level.

The notion of merchant banks and their role has not been the same in the United States and the United Kingdom as in France, Japan, and West Germany. British and American merchant banks are essentially brokers who act as catalysts in the shifts of capital distribution but (with the exception of S. G. Warburg and Lazard) take little interest in industrial strategy or in industry's future. They therefore facilitate equity redistribution but are little concerned with conditions favorable to the internal growth of firms. This financial approach preferred by most merchant banks contrasts with industrial strategy, where growth by acquisition is the exception, as illustrated by the Japanese model and, to a lesser extent, the German and Swiss models. In these countries, merchant banking departments of banks operate in the context of a longer-term outlook where the ultimate priority is industrial development rather than short-term financial profitability.

The diversity of these banking systems can also be evaluated in terms of the degree of concentration of the financial system. Once again, Japan is a case on its own because of the role of the large commercial banks. As time goes on, there will probably be a move toward greater concentration of the Japanese banking system. The regional banks will most likely end up participating in a federation, on what will certainly be diverse and multiple terms, with the large Tokyo banks; this will enable them to address their problems of international outlets and scale economies.

Such a concentration might be encouraged by the Japanese public authorities. Several systems of alliance will certainly exist side by side, depending on whether Daiwa, Nomura, or Yamachi joins in an alliance with banks or insurance companies. The banking licenses obtained in London by Daiwa and Nomura could favor closer co-operation with insurance companies and therefore enable them to compete with global banks, particularly the Japanese ones. They would then have the means: access to long-term resources, investment and placing capacity, distribution network, computer system, and captive private customers.

The prospects for reorganization, determined as they are by

the pecularities of national banking systems, are probably greater in Japan than in European countries such as France or West Germany. For a century now, the banking structure in West Germany has been very stable, with its concept of "Universal Bank," and commercial banks also performing operations in general reserved for merchant banks in the United Kingdom or the United States. France has recently made extensive changes in the rules for the functioning of monetary and financial markets and the extension of credit, with interest rate subsidies and greatly modified management of the public debt and the status of the main participants. These measures are principally aimed at putting an end to the partitioning of the market between monetary and financial activities, and to the over-regulation of this market, where bond issues, commission scales and brokerage tables, foreign investments, and credit restrictions were all subject to regulation. All this made real competition impossible on a market where the financial intermediaries themselves defined market agreements. Accordingly, a set of measures was adopted in order to unify the capital markets, to open them up to all economic agents, and to create forward markets for securities previously negotiated on the spot market and on numerous maturity dates.

This has had the following results:

1 Certificates of deposit were created in March 1985 in order to enable banks to borrow on the short-term securities market, which are negotiable with all investors.
2 Commercial paper can now be issued by firms which need cash.
3 Negotiable Treasury bonds put an end to bilateral public financing by allowing the state to issue securities to which all economic agents can subscribe.
4 The reform of the mortgage market has enabled financing to be ensured for all economic agents. This is long-term and simple financing, managed by an agency which continuously issues long-maturity bonds listed on the stock exchange, which by eliminating traditional mismatching reduces the cost of the resources obtained in this manner.

5 The futures market in financial instruments has enabled the creation of cover on markets which previously only existed on the spot market. Futures contracts are therefore of the utmost importance for covering financial exposures (hedging).
6 It is now possible to take options on markets where before only a firm commitment was possible.

Elements of world supervision: New risks and new forms of control

One priority is imperative: supervision of banks must allow assessment of the quality of the long-term strategy of the institutions to be controlled. The reason for this is that, as in all industries that are both labor- and capital-intensive, increased productivity, the dissemination of new technologies, and innovation takes place over a long period of time, often ten to fifteen years.

Assessing strategy: The choice of indicators

For most banks, probably the most important indicator is the level of net margin before provisions, related to the size and nature of the risks assumed. Numerous factors influence net margin: the evolution of general expenses, commissions collected, the differential between interest expenses and interest income, and profits arising from trading financial instruments and foreign exchange. The fact remains that in the end the net margin constitutes the first and main line of defense against economic risk.

The level of equity must be determined so as to take into account current and future risks with which the banks are and will be confronted. These are linked to industrial and agricultural transformation and to the serious difficulties encountered by developing countries with their foreign debt; and they are heightened by the development of new activities and by the evolution of legal decisions in the area of fiduciary liability which may soon make the banks increasingly accountable for the results obtained for their customers in managing the capital entrusted to them.

The amount of capital required to cover possible loan losses cannot be rigorously fixed in advance. No one has yet found the ideal ratio which makes it possible to assess a bank's solvency.[12]

The public authorities will probably change the ways in which they exercise their supervisory activity. Quantitative control will be maintained by encouraging the banks to reinforce their equity gradually according to the nature of the risks assumed. Liquidity ratios and maximum commitment levels per debtor will have to be kept, and probably extended to cover bank and country risks. There will in addition be a trend toward qualitative control which strives to assess the strategy of each institution in terms of human and capital resources available to them, and a gradual introduction of standard accounting rules, in particular for the handling of provisions and reserves, and depreciation of computer expenses and other investments.

All supervisors assessing the degree of a bank's solvency face a permanent choice between book value and the liquidation value. In the framework of day-to-day supervision, it is probably not desirable to accord convertible loan securities or other forms of debt based on specific agreements (perpetual subordinated debt) the same importance as true equity because they can only cover losses in the case of liquidation. Whether or not unpublished reserves are included in a bank's shareholder equity varies considerably from one country to another. Indeed, in contrast to the United Kingdom, many countries allow general reserves to be deducted from the tax base. The reserves, moreover, have very different roles, depending on whether they cover risks of imminent losses or whether their only goal is to influence the tax position favorably.

However, experience shows that over a long period of time, the market assesses the company's real wealth. On the whole, the difference, if there is one, between the net value of assets and market capitalization gives a fairly accurate picture of the degree of a bank's provision, whether excessive or insufficient. It is true that the existence of hidden reserves makes evaluation and comparison of the financial situations of different banks more difficult for the market. But by the same token, it must be admitted that these reserves can play an important role if there is a danger of a loss of confidence in the bank.

Generally speaking, assessment of a bank's solvency supposes that the following questions have been answered. Is it possible to measure adequately a bank's shareholder equity? How can the various risks be assessed? Must quantitative standards be imposed for all operators? The method used in most countries to evaluate risk consists in laying down standard ratios relating a bank's shareholder equity to its total commitments and weighted by the degree of risk taken for each type of asset.

In combination with or as an alternative to this method, some countries use a ratio of the bank's shareholder equity to liabilities. The primary advantage of a system of this kind is its simplicity. It enables members of the public to reach an assessment for themselves, using the balance sheets published by the bank. On the other hand, it obviously does not take into consideration the risk in the bank's assets: it would be possible with this method to reach a similar evaluation of two banks, one investing exclusively in government bonds and the other in high-risk credits.

An equally important tool in assessing risks is the large exposures rule, which places a limit on loans to counterparties on the basis of the banks' available equity. The percentage varies, again, depending on the country.

Risk and solvency: Alternative approaches

When studying the solvency of financial institutions, a link must be established between the system for assessing risks and the system for checking solvency. The British authorities have shown some flexibility in defining quantitative standards which take into consideration the specific conditions and particular situation of each bank. In the United States, the method is less flexible. It is principally based on assessing the relative position of each institution within its peer group. The most radical system is based on a purely quantitative method applied to all banks, regardless of their size or their individual nature. Finally, a middle-of-the-road approach, such as that in The Netherlands, combines these systems. This method leaves considerable scope for pragmatism in the application of criteria. The regulatory requirements of solvency are used only as indicators, not as a measure of whether the bank is functioning correctly. Other factors come into play when assessing the degree of management efficiency, such as the competence of senior management, the consistency and rigor of accounting practices, and the quality of the loan portfolio. For this reason, the Central Bank of The Netherlands requires a specific provision when the quality of a loan is considered doubtful. This is deducted from the bank's shareholder equity, therefore from the bank's liabilities.

The advantages of the quantitative method, applied indiscriminately to all banks, are well known. It is conducive to self-discipline, forcing the banks to maintain their capital at levels fixed by norms; and it ensures a certain transparency in the banking system by providing objective comparisons. Nevertheless, there are obvious drawbacks to this system. The establishment of these norms remains somewhat arbitrary and does not sufficiently take into account qualitative factors; and it is difficult with this method to establish a mass of valid international experience, given that assets and reserves are evaluated differently in different countries.

The long trend toward the decline of the bank solvency ratios[13] made an about-turn several years ago in face of increased risks. Since then, banks have considerably improved their equity ratios by means of retained earnings, the building up of reserves of a general nature, and the issue of shares and new instruments which have the legal characteristics of equity (life subrogated bonds). It is difficult to strike a perfect balance between the different components of equity. It is safe to say, however, that the larger a bank's net margin, the better it is placed to hold a sizeable fraction of equity in subordinated term debt. According to an OECD study, at the beginning of the nineteenth century capital stood at 40 percent of total liabilities, since when it has been in decline – a very abrupt decline in some countries in recent years.

In numerous industrial countries, the ratio of equity to debt for industrial corporations has deteriorated, in some extreme cases from 1:1 to 1:3. This increases the risk for banks accordingly, and therefore leads to a greater need for equity in order to offset the relative undermining of their solvency.

However, the banks' ability to raise equity in sufficient quantities is limited by the fact that in many cases their market value is approximately equal to or often below the value of net assets. The main reasons for this are the international debt crisis, the need for a high level of provisions for doubtful debts linked to the financing of leveraged buy-outs and property transactions, and the risks and challenges inherent in foreign competition and the implementation of information technology. These factors have resulted in numerous banks seeing their shares quoted below net asset value, making it very difficult for them to perform the necessary capital increases.

Current priorities

Under current conditions, the banks and supervisory authorities find themselves faced with three questions:[14]

1 Considering the risks, what should the level of equity be to ensure depositor protection?
2 Should equity, reserves, subordinated bonds, and perpetual and convertible subordinated bonds be placed on equal footing? Must these continue to have the same weighting ratios?
3 Should the supervisory bodies exercise control over credit and other financial activities initiated by the non-financial sector, and if so, in what form?

The Cooke Report, prepared by the Bank for International Settlements Committee on Banking Regulation and Supervisory Practice, provides answers to the first two of these questions.

In banking, as in other economic sectors, growth depends on the mobilization of sufficient resources in capital and their effective use, even if the role of capital has changed. Capital can be defined as all the funds belonging to the bank's owners in the form of ordinary and preferential shares, to which must be added reserves published in the balance sheet. In the past, a bank had to have capital in order to assume credit risks. Today, securitization of a large percentage of credits displaces the problem of the theoretical allocation of capital. It seems paradoxical that just when securitization is beginning to develop, when the statistical risk is being largely covered by the margin charged to the individual, and when financial assets are assuming a greater role in the balance sheet, the central banks are co-ordinating their actions to force banks to increase their equity.

Two hypotheses might explain this. Each of them is valid in part:

1 The supervisory bodies have realized somewhat belatedly the extent of undercapitalization of the large banks and have adopted measures to solve difficulties which have changed in nature.
2 The nature of the risks associated with money-market activities defies assessment. The size of the volumes handled, the complexity of new products, the more or less widespread discrepancy between both internal and external control and the implementation of these new products place the banks in a situation comparable to that of the insurance sector at the beginning of commercial aviation. Thus, when in doubt, security is favored.

In recent years, banks' equity needs have grown to unprecedented levels with the enlargement of financial markets and the growth of banking firms in an inflationary environment. Expansion of the banking sector has accelerated and its services have diversified, as indicated by developments in overseas representation and presence on international currency and securities markets. These trends have transformed the structure of the bank's balance sheet: the new diversity of banking operations and the multitude of risks have led to consolidation. Although the degree of consolidation may differ from one country to another, the importance of equity levels is now recognized everywhere. Indeed, all banks need shareholder equity to cover their fixed assets and risk investments, to continue growth, and to maintain their depositors' confidence, particularly in the event of a crisis. The required level of a bank's shareholder equity varies from country to country according to historical factors. In West Germany and Japan, where the banks have played an important role in the long-term financing of industry, shareholders' equity ratios are higher than in the United States, where the system remains tied to major regulatory constraints, themselves elaborated to a large extent in the light of lessons drawn from the great depression of the 1930s. However, the past twenty years have undeniably seen national differences between banking institutions and ranges of services becoming blurred, reflecting the internationalization and growing interdependence of the world of finance. Many banks have evolved toward multispeciality, operating both on domestic and international markets; the same factors which contribute to intensifying competition between banks make the system more efficient.

The concept of liquidity is an important one because it enables a link to be established between capital and confidence. However, the liquidity constraint has changed in nature. Securitization has modified the management of a bank's liquidity. It must, nevertheless, still be managed according to the composition and quality of the bank's assets, within the norms imposed by the supervisory bodies. This nature of liquidity was underscored by G. Rae,[15] who believes that the soundness of a bank depends on its capital, and that its immediate security depends on its degree of liquidity. Back in the nineteenth century, banks' liquid assets were held in the form of cash, commercial bills, and other short-term securities negotiated on the money market, with the ratio of liquid assets to deposits at around 30 percent. The amount and structure of these liquid assets evolved over time. Treasury bonds became a liquid asset in World War I and have remained so ever since.

In the period between the two World Wars, clearing banks had to adhere to two ratios which were considered important: a published ratio of 10 percent cash; and a second ratio – for internal use – of money-market assets, of which 30 percent comprised first-class securities. The liquidity ratio was changed to 8 percent after World War II and became a formal requirement of the authorities for monetary control purposes in the 1950s. These provisions, apart from a few changes, remained in force until 1971, when proposals from the Bank of England on "Competition and Credit Control" began to alter the landscape. Beginning in 1971, the clearing banks could adjust their liquidity by borrowing and lending on the wholesale market. The normal strategy of a cautious bank treasurer was then to lend on this market any excess amount and to borrow as little as possible in order to cover temporary liquidity needs.

Under these conditions, the existence of a lender of last resort remained essential to system's stability. In London and Paris, this role was always played by the Bank of England and the Bank of France respectively, whereas on international currency markets, the Bank for International Settlements fulfilled an important function as co-ordinator of interventions by central banks.

4

◇

The Human Resources Constraint

◆

HUMAN RESOURCES: THE BACKGROUND

Banking is a world industry whose main protagonists are the Japanese, the British, the Americans, and the Europeans. The struggle for financial power conceals a latent confrontation of minds, of cultures, and often of opposing ideas. The dynamism of the Japanese, American, and British financial industries has its roots in philosophies of management which to a Frenchman, for example, can appear just as unreal and poorly suited to France's national temperament as the style of direct and rigorous management of American industrialists in the post-World War II period. Yet over the past forty years, a considerable shift in the British and European mentality has occurred, in which the spirit of enterprise, the working of free competition, the development of international activities are among the most important elements. But it seems necessary to go far beyond this to meet the challenge of the forthcoming decades. Fundamentally, Europeans, in the broad sense of the word, must once again learn to revitalize forward-looking analysis; to redefine the concept of efficiency, no longer limiting it, for example, to the mere streamlining of personnel but widening it to embrace the notions of personal commitment and communication; to understand that to govern is to obtain the approval of executives and of employees, and that decision without implementation never changed reality; to realize that for a project to become reality it must receive input from the entire organization – in short, to recognize that future banking strategy requires qualitative transformations.

The human resources constraint deserves, above any other constraint, specific consideration in any analysis of banking strategy. In quantitative terms, we need to look at how employment in banks has evolved and to consider the causes, the extent, and the nature of overstaffing. In qualitative terms, addressing the composition of the staff, we must aim to transform the skills required and modify the decision-making process in order to meet the challenge launched by competing banks and financial institutions.

QUANTITATIVE ASPECTS

In banking, as in industry, the evolution of technology and environmental constraints have resulted in overstaffing, which in France, the United Kingdom, Italy, and Japan can be estimated at between 25 percent and 35 percent (compared with the 1985 level). In fact, the banks will be forced, on average and over a period of fifteen years, to reduce their staff by 35 percent and recruit 10 percent.

The information revolution and the dissemination of knowledge, when aimed at lowering the cost of production, causes contractions in the producer sectors – in this case banking – and in the adjacent sectors linked to them. The ultimate consequence of innovation is therefore a liberation of the work-force, the terms and pace of which are determined by banks' strategic choices and the means adopted by their senior officers to implement them.

Today's situation: The end of a long trend

Banking is a heavily capitalized industry whose investments consist essentially of employees, to such an extent that the transformations required can only be effected over time. History has shown that accelerated increases in employment have frequently occurred in reaction to a pressing demand from customers, in particular in the period following World War II. However, only very few institutions initiated in the 1970s a strategy which sought to anticipate market changes and to prepare people for these transformations by bringing in a large number of executives. Consequently, few of them have understood the implications for their staff of recent fundamental shifts, such as the explosion of information technology and its effects on the configuration of branch networks and on money and data transmission flows, securitization and its impact on credit distribution and on risk analysis, and the changing role of foreign branches.

Rather than devoting their talents to implementing practical solutions which would have gradually modified the number and composition of the work-force, many banks opted for the leverage effect, accumulating assets at margins that were often insufficient to remunerate their capital, but that were sufficient to ensure a temporary increase in gross profits. At the same time, these banks began to invest in advanced technologies and services, resulting in numerous cases in overheads increasing at an alarming pace.

Today's overstaffing is the result of this lack of strategic reflection and the shortcomings of the decision-implementing process these past twenty years. In banking, cultural factors make the move from the planning stage to real action extremely difficult, especially if problems of structure and organization are involved. Banks, protected by national regulations, settled into situations of high profit-yielding monopolies, which even recently still tended to attract executives who were more interested in maintaining the status quo than involving themselves in adopting new technologies and promoting them at all levels with daily training.

It is worth looking at what happened in the United States. American banks, dominating the international banking world, have been the most sensitive to these new requirements in human resource management and also the first to react. The rationalization of certain tasks and the restructuring which they carried out were transmitted to the international banks in an oligopolistic environment where efforts to introduce competition must continue if the banks are not to go under. The trend to reduce jobs in the banking sector in the United States[1] was the forerunner of transformations at world level.

Four factors explain the increase in US bank employment up to the 1970s.

1 The role of banks in the economy has continued to be asserted, as attested by the growth of bank assets above that of GNP. Parallel to this, the number of employees recruited to manage these assets increased at a time when the technological revolution had not yet called into question the link between growth and employment.[2]
2 The continued rise in interest rates and the growing volatility of financial markets contributed to the growth of trading activities, as well as of the traditional cash and portfolio management functions.
3 The volume of transactions has increased more consistently than GNP or international trade. According to a study by the Bank Administration Institute, the volume of checks handled in the United States grew at an annual 7 percent in the 1970s while the use of credit cards increased even more rapidly.[3]
4 In an effort to distinguish themselves from others, and because "Regulation Q" limited the amount of interest that could be paid on certain deposits, banks increased the number of services offered to depositors and opened more branches.

Thus, the increased volume of transactions and the effects of "Regulation Q" favored the creation of many jobs: and of every ten new jobs, seven involved the handling of checks and customer management. Then, in the mid-1970s, this upward trend in staff suddenly went into reverse. Three factors appear to have played a determining role in this change.

1 The elimination of "Regulation Q" reintroduced competition in the area of bank deposit yields. This in turn reduced the need to have branches throughout a region. One year after

the Monetary Control Act had allowed interest to be paid on current accounts, the number of branch openings had declined.[4] Between 1958 and 1975, an average of 1,500 branches were set up every year; in 1983, 1,000. After 1984 the number tended to level off at about 500.

2 Automated payment systems were introduced.

3 New competitors entering areas traditionally reserved for the banks had their effect on the level and distribution of staff.

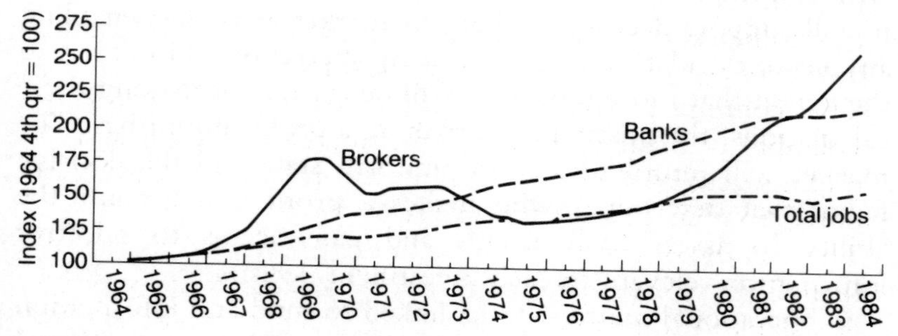

FIGURE 4.1 Employment growth in banking, 1964–1984
Source: National Bureau of Economic Research; United States Department of Labor, Bureau of Labor Statistics

Certain bank functions were gradually taken over by brokers, pension funds, even industrial firms. According to a study by the United States Department of Labor, between the first quarter of 1981 and the second quarter of 1984, in a new period of full competition, employment grew by 18 percent in the Savings and Loans Associations against 5 percent in the banks.[5]

Forecasts: Technological progress and new jobs

How the problem of overstaffing is tackled in the sector in the years to come will depend on two related phenomena. On the one hand, new forms of market activities, service provision, and portfolio management will generate jobs. On the other hand, the substitution of capital for labor will continue, doing away with repetitive tasks or tasks with little value added, which will eliminate an increasingly large number of jobs. However, wage costs will tend to remain steady, because average salaries will be higher as more jobs will require technical skills and a larger proportion of salaries will be results related.

Within the next decade or so, artificial intelligence is expected to be capable of handling most of the work which is at present essentially administrative, that is, which has very little to do with communication or the effective exercise of responsibilities. It will support decision-making in market activities, enabling anyone to calculate temporary pricing aberrations. However, to the extent that more operators will be capable of making these calculations, the possibility of making a profit diminishes. The market will return to a more uniform state and the decisive factor that determines who makes a profit will become the ability to assess basic trends and gain access to selective information relevant to each investment decision.

In operational matters, tasks linked to fund and information movements will be handled largely through the use of artificial intelligence. An individual will be able, from the keyboard, to enter the financial characteristics of his or her household into the central computer and ask the computer to provide the most appropriate financial assets, taking into account the household's propensity to save and its aversion to risk, without there being any advice on managing these assets at this stage. The expert system will in this case replace intervention by specialists. A similar evolution could occur to that in medicine in certain regions of the United States, where computers answer emergency medical calls from patients who inform them of their symptoms in order to determine whether or not hospitalization is necessary.

Computerization has not protected sectors which traditionally create employment. Take the case of investment securities. Here, employment rose in the 1960s mainly on account of the increased volume of business. Since that time processing procedures have been modernized and the industry itself has undergone computerization. All these innovations have enabled the New York Stock Exchange to achieve over a period of twenty years a growth rate for its volume of transactions ten times greater than the growth rate of employment. A similar trend has been observed in the brokerage business for private clients, which though in principle it requires the largest work-force, has today a negative impact on job growth. This trend is chiefly due to the displacement of individual investors by institutions who, either on their own account or for the account of customers grouped together in unit trusts, have turned most stock markets into wholesale markets. The result has been economies of scale and therefore reduced employment.

The evolution of the work-force within a bank is closely linked to the quest for productivity which can be defined in terms of a vulnerability ratio between the net operating income and overhead cost. Productivity gains can be determined by analyzing overhead items and calculating their real added value in terms of customer service, risk control, or risk reduction. This is done, of course, within the framework of a clearly defined plan and strategies consistent with this plan. From this position, arbitrages are carried out, transferring operating and employee expenses from sectors where administrative tasks account for most of the activity to other wealth-creating centers which correspond to the customer's future needs. Global figures therefore reflect these trends only in part. The work-force evolved in this manner,[6] in most industrialized countries, from the 1960s to the mid-1970s. In 1977, the average growth rate, varying between countries, was between 3 percent and 7 percent. This rate has since then not been negative, even in such countries as Spain. Studies by the International Federation of Employees, Technicians and Managers of eleven European countries confirm the downturn in the second half of the 1970s. Figures for 1986 revealed very sluggish growth, even reductions in staff in France and Denmark and a steady decline in most countries to 1990.

A look at employment growth rates in three categories of banks (large banks, commercial banks, and savings banks) reveals a net increase in jobs until 1987 in The Netherlands (mainly due to commercial banks), in the United Kingdom

TABLE 4.1 Annual growth rate of banking jobs by country, 1986 (%)

Country	*Large banks*	*Commercial banks*	*Savings banks*
Canada	4·09		
Finland	–	2·13	
France	0·23		
Greece	3·20		
Italy	3·75	4·78	4·10
The Netherlands		11·77	0·49
Portugal			
Sweden		0·26	1·73
Switzerland		5·56	4·85[a]
United Kingdom			9·56
United States			4·05
Spain	1·54	1·69	7·05
Yugoslavia		11·16	

[a] Cantons.

(building societies), in Italy, and in Switzerland, where employment is growing uniformly for all financial institutions (see table 4.1). Sweden is in a stable position thanks to its relatively mature banking industry. Also since 1987, a trend toward staff reductions of 1–3 percent per year can be seen in the United States, Europe, and Japan.

In terms of employment, the recent trend, which coming years will probably confirm, is characterized by:

- a decrease in staff, not necessarily accompanied by a reduction in wage costs;
- a change in the structure of the work-force in line with the need to improve and enlarge the range of skills at all levels;
- a different approach to human resources, with emphasis not only on technical skills but also on behavior, teamwork, and innovation.

However, the decline in the number of employees is a result of contradictory movements. The effects of rationalizing repetitive tasks, competition from non-bank institutions, and fewer jobs in trading could be partially offset by the provision of new services such as management of pension funds and private wealth, intermediation in the securitization of debts, and new forms of export and industrial investment aid.

Nevertheless, the net change in staff globally will be negative, except for a few institutions which began organizing this process of adaptation long ago, and which placed support for industry at the heart of their strategy: for the growth potential of that area is almost unlimited, bringing with it a need for qualified staff that will grow in proportion to industrial expansion.

QUALITATIVE ASPECTS

If banks are to be successful in the near future they will have to redefine the principle of human resource management and make this one of the top priorities of their senior officers. What is at stake goes far beyond quantity. It concerns the composition of the staff and its capacity to mobilize itself at all levels to implement the bank's strategic intentions in order to meet the challenge of the next decade.[7]

In most institutions the percentage of managers and employees devoted to administrative and repetitive tasks is probably much too high compared with the customers' present and future needs. On the other hand, there are too few qualified people capable of developing and implementing new software, of providing support to the industrial clients to help them achieve their strategy, and of obtaining convincing results over a long period of time in project financing and private wealth management. One of the ways of remedying this lack is by reorienting the banks' priorities to make them more sensitive to customers' needs and then introducing a profit-sharing mechanism, based jointly on individual performance and on the overall results achieved by the institution. These schemes must encourage actions which contribute to the bank's long-term development, favor team solidarity, and stimulate each and every employee to achieve his or her maximum performance in the light of the institution's strategic priorities as well as its annual objectives.

The reciprocity of people and structures

A bank's success is not ensured only by the presence of high-performing managers, but also by the choices made about organization and structure. The financial world is a turbulent one, with prices constantly altering and a rapid pace of change. In order to cope with this, it is essential that all in a bank, from the junior employees to the senior officers, are *fully* involved. This cannot be achieved without a change in management philosophy enabling each and every one to assume fully the responsibilities allotted to him or her and to provide the concrete solutions which contribute to the bank's competitiveness as a whole.

The solution lies in a move toward a decentralized modular structure, enabling more refined market analyses, for example, by distinguishing individuals, in terms of socio-professional category, income level, geographical distribution, and age group in order to create the best targeted products. This can only be the work of small specialized teams with close and often informal links of collaboration. New advances in information technology will make this type of structure not only possible but indispensable.

Implementation of a structure which is in step with the strategy is a must for any reform and reflects the will to adapt and to come out on top in a changing environment: within the bank, new jobs emerge, specialization comes into play, and customers, from the private individual to the large firm, demand that their needs be met globally. In order to respond to the diversity of these requirements and yet maintain an identity and specific approach, each bank must have a strategy, consistent with the bank's culture, which enables patterns of thought and knowledge to be combined and a common language developed, without which there can be no shared vision.

First of all, the bank's senior officers, the real inducers of change, must diagnose the institution's strengths and weaknesses, the environment's opportunities and threats. They must then develop a clear vision of the mission and strategic intent of their organization. A long-term plan must then outline the necessary changes in technology, human resources, equity, management structures, communication, and control. Finally, there comes the most important phase: implementation, for strategy *is* implementation.

In order for this process to unfold gradually, the bank must minimize conflicts between the bank's different functions, in particular between those which have different methods of remuneration and between the generations: these are bound to be acute, given the contrast between banking as it was practiced fifteen years ago and as it will be practiced tomorrow. In the corporate world of the last fifty years the pace of change has been slower within banking than in most other industries – probably because of the relatively protected environment they have hitherto enjoyed. Now most banks are having to deal with significant internal organizational questions as well as with cultural issues associated with conflicts between generations.[8]

We can say with March and Simon that "conflict applies to a blocking of normal decision-making mechanisms, so that an individual or a group encounters difficulty in choosing its action."[9] Or, with Wilemon and Thamhain: "The behavior of an individual, a group or an organization is said to be conflictual if it prevents or hinders, at least temporarily, the possibility for another individual, group or organization to reach the goals it has set for itself. The conflict can be disjunctive if it leads to disintegration of the collective effort or blocks the decision-making process."[10] These definitions place greater emphasis on the organizational aspect than Hill's,[11] which could be qualified as relational: "Conflict can be defined as an interpersonal incompatibility. Most of the social conflicts are of a relational nature, that is, they only appear when two or several people work or live together."

It is possible to identify three sources of conflict:

1 Poor management of the diversity–identity ratio within the bank, where the traditional culture has not absorbed new values and the influx of people linked with the need to introduce a faster pace of change.

2 Absence of a shared company vision, with no real consensus on the bank's purpose and its specific role in the financial world and in its domestic market. The result is serious difficulties in allocating scarce human and capital resources.
3 Ambiguity in the rules of the game, particularly those relating to the decision-making process.

A typology similar to that of Clagett Smith[12] is also worth mentioning:

1 problems of communication between two parts of the organization;
2 opposing interests or objectives between two parts;
3 absence of a community of perceptions or attitudes between members of the organization's different levels.

New internal conflicts

Market activities versus administrative tasks

The essential characteristics of a management style conducive to implementing a plan of action are the sense that a direct influence is being exercised on the course of events; the ability to assume responsibilities that have tangible results; and the link between assuming responsibility and the final result, in terms of individual recognition and financial reward – both of which remain extremely important.

The internationalization of capital markets has led to an internationalization of the management and remuneration methods used by market operators. Experience has shown that small teams of managers who are interested in results, who have been given real decision-making autonomy and who are subject to strict controls, today constitute the most efficient means of management. The most successful banks have set up teams organized on this principle. Other institutions, which have deferred introducing major reform, have created subsidiaries where the best performing operators are grouped together so that there is no longer the need to manage the necessary changes from within.

Although the banks have had to make major changes in their organizational and human resource management to be competitive on the capital market, only a few have extended and adapted this reform to other sectors. Two of these are Citicorp and the Deutsche Bank, which have grouped together all activities of the same type in profit centers endowed with a large degree of autonomy for risk assumption, new product and customer development, and information technology investments. Moreover, they have implemented profit-sharing schemes based not only on direct profits but on contributions to the profitability of other sectors and on results obtained for customers, in order to keep the range of action and behavior within bounds.

If this method of management is to be extended throughout an entire institution, it is essential that authority is delegated to the lowest possible levels, thus modifying the decision-making process. If this is not done, the bank will break up into two opposed factions, one comprised of entrepreneurs interested in results, the other made up of fixed-wage earners who execute orders handed down from above. If this happens, the bank's ability to respond to changes would risk being called into question by the departure of its most dynamic elements. Already, some of the most talented executives in trading activities, software development, and management of private wealth have set up their own businesses as consultants or middlemen outside the main structure.

The lack of a shared vision and of a strong organizational culture have resulted in many banks becoming fragmented and having lost many of their best people.

Some of the large American and European banks have been able to adapt to changes in the market by focusing their attention on three major areas: personal banking, wholesale banking, and money-market banking. They have created light structures which enable small, high-quality teams to make decisions that are very close to the customer. Citicorp was the first to adopt this type of organization, with the European banks then imitating it and the Japanese banks adopting certain concepts but adjusting them to their own cultural environment.

The conflict between generations

In addition to the conflict between functions within a bank nature, there also exists a conflict between the methods used to exercise authority.

In the thirty years after World War II, banking grew in a way compatible with a centralized decision-making process, and in order to ensure bank expansion, jobs had to be created all the time. Today, the entire industry built up in this period of unrelenting growth, finds itself in an awkward position. Banks who reject the challenge to their established practices are forced to retreat to a position where they significantly scale down the scope of their activities to adapt them to their management practices. To become a world bank, different management methods must be implemented, even if a culture where every member participates is difficult to introduce in institutions with a mentality deeply embedded in the oldest methods of organization known to Western man, namely extreme centralism and individualism.

By the end of this decade, in order to have any chance of a lasting position among the world's top fifty banks, a bank must adopt a style of management which contributes to the durability and efficiency of the firm by allowing each and every individual to become a player in areas traditionally reserved for senior management: strategic planning, organization, promotion, development, and control. This means creating a living body made up of numerous decision centers with real responsibilities, using a common language and thinking patterns in order to ensure real communication and lasting commitment to achieve the shared strategic goal.

It is becoming clear that the human resources constraint, even if the process of change is slower because of the need to modify habits and behavior, takes precedence over all the others – technological, financial, regulatory, commercial. Moreover, it controls the technological constraint, which, thanks to data processing and artificial intelligence, will continue to reshape the banking world at an unprecedented pace provided that men and women have been properly prepared for their implementation.

It can not be overstated that for tomorrow's banks, more than ever before because of the Japanese, the most important investment will be in recruiting, training, and stimulating people. A bank's investment policy can be summed up for the most part as a human resource program implemented within the framework of a clear strategy.

PART II

STRATEGIC CHOICES

5

◇

The Evolution of Banking Structures: The United States, Europe, and Japan

◆

THE SHAPE OF EVOLUTION

Since the beginning of the 1970s, the world's leading banks have had to cope with two major factors shaping their destiny: the instability of the environment and the sector's degree of maturity. Far from feeling confident that their position in the world hierarchy is secure, they are faced with a choice: either expand or die.

The reinforcement of the international financial system in an increasingly unstable environment has favored a redistribution of roles and has heightened the volatility of the decision-making risk for those in charge. Considerable change in the banking hierarchy has been brought about by the transformation of the balance of power between industrialized economies and the increased risk attached to Western commercial bank commitments in developing countries. A look at these shifts in the hierarchy reveals two main phenomena: growth and concentration.

The growth of the banking sector

The rapid growth in total assets held by the world's 300 leading banks is an indication of the banking sector's increased power within the economies of industrialized countries. Between 1973 and 1988, the assets of the top 300 banks grew from $2,223 bn to $15,431 bn – a growth rate nearly twice as fast as that of world GDP, which rose from $4,078 bn to $15,000 bn over the same period. The multiplying coefficient of these assets expressed in dollars was 3.5 between 1973 and 1985, increasing to 6.9 in the period from 1973 to 1988. There has therefore clearly been a very strong upward movement since 1985.

Depreciation of the dollar in relation to the other major currencies since 1985 is undoubtedly one of the major reasons for this acceleration. A look at the structure of the banking system on a country-by-country basis shows that Japan has continued to consolidate its position. Of the ten leading banks in 1988, 9 were Japanese, whereas only one was present in 1979 and none were to be seen in 1969. The 1980s have been a time of Japanese self-assertion in the banking world. This ascendancy of course also means that those banks which previously made up the core of the world banking system have found themselves consigned to less enviable positions. The most abrupt descent in the hierarchy was that of the American banks, which, having held seven of the ten leading positions in 1969, were reduced to two in 1979 and none at all in 1988 (though Citicorp appeared in eleventh place).

The European banks had their day at the top of the banking structure in the interim period between the decline of the

TABLE 5.1 Distribution of assets of 300 leading banks, by country, 1973–1988 ($bn)

Country	*1973*	*1988*	*Growth, 1973–1988*
Japan	420	5,665	13·49
France	142	1,317	9·27
Switzerland	56	335	5·98
West Germany	259	1,420	5·48
Italy	163	769	4·72
United Kingdom	168	744	4·42
United States	574	1,664	2·90
Others	441	3,217	7·29
Total	2,223	15,131	6·81

Source: *The Banker*, 1974, 1989.

TABLE 5.2 Top fifteen banks 1988–1989, showing Japan's leadership in terms of total assets, but its weak ratio equity/balance sheet total (no allowance made for hidden reserves)

Name of bank	*Country*	*Total assets ($bn)*	*Total equity ($bn)*	*Ratio of total equity to total assets (%)*
Dai Ichi Kangyo Bank	Japan[a]	386·94[b]	10·95	2·83
Sumitomo Bank	Japan	376·09	10·46	2·78
Fuji Bank	Japan	364·04	10·73	2·95
Sanwa Bank	Japan	348·36	9·31	2·67
Mitsubishi Bank	Japan	343·59	9·68	2·82
Industrial Bank of Japan	Japan	257·58	8·57	3·33
Norin Chukin Bank	Japan	241·95	1·38	0·57
Tokai Bank	Japan	225·12	6·16	2·74
Mitsui Bank	Japan	219·67	5·77	2·63
Mitsubishi Trust	Japan	210·47	5·13	2·44
Crédit agricole	France	207·99	9·03	4·34
Citicorp	United States	203·83	9·86	4·84
Sumitomo Trust	Japan	196·59	4·69	2·39
Banque nationale de Paris	France	194·52	5·50	2·83
Barclays plc	United Kingdom	189·20	10·32	5·46

[a] Figure for the Japanese banks are as of 31 March 1989.
[b] Exchange rates are those in effect as of 31 December 1988.
Source: *American Banker*, 31 December 1988.

American empire and the rise of Japanese domination. Between 1973 and 1988, the number of Japanese banks in the top 300 rose from fifty-two to seventy-four while their assets increased by a multiple of over 13. However, if the exchange effect of the 100 percent appreciation of the yen against the dollar during this period is taken into consideration, the increase in Japanese bank assets comes out at just a little over fivefold (5.35). The number of European banks among the leading 300 remained steady at 132; however, within this, the number of British banks declined and the number of West German banks rose. The quantitative drop of American banks from eighty-three to forty-three is an indication of the downward trend of the entire American banking sector, not of a crisis restricted to the large US money center banks. The US geographical area has had the lowest rate

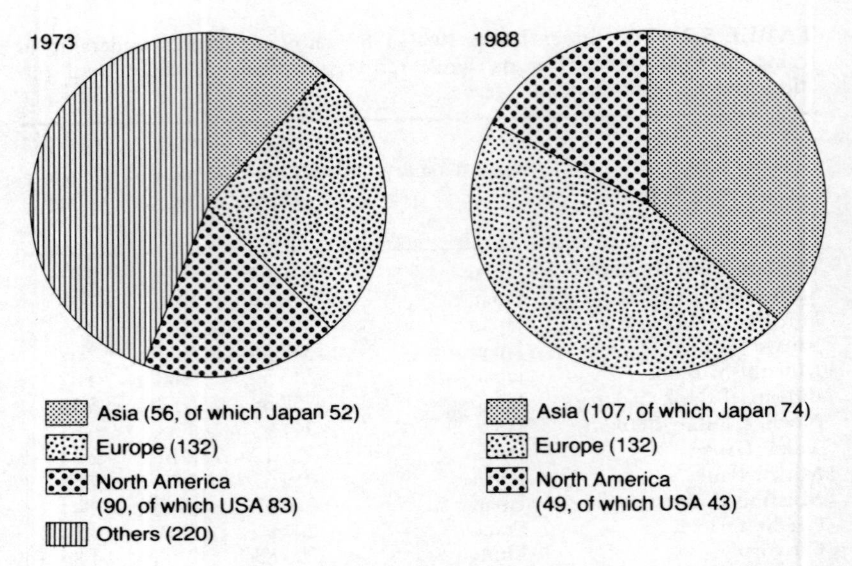

FIGURE 5.1 Geographical distribution of the world top 300 banks, 1973 and 1988
Source: *The Banker*

TABLE 5.3 Distribution of 300 leading banks and assets, by country, 1986–1988, with growth of assets 1973–1988

Region/country	*No. of banks*		*Assets ($bn)*		*Growth of assets, 1973–88*
	1986	*1988*	*1986*	*1988*	
North America	90	49	661	2,015	3·05
United States	56	43	574	1,664	2·90
Europe	132	132	1,021	6,107	5·98
France	13	14	142	1,317	9·27
West Germany	29	32	259	1,420	5·48
United Kingdom	15	10	168	744	4·42
Asia	56	107	438	6,651	15·18
Japan	22	12	103	5,665	13·49
Others	22	12	103	359	3·49
Total	300	300	2,223	15,431	6·94

Source: *The Banker*, 1987, 1989.

of growth in assets, remaining, in constant dollars, 50 percent below that of the Japanese banks.

The evolving structure of the banking sector has also seen the emergence of strong banking centers in the Middle East and in Pacific Asia. This is the result of the integration of these regions in the world economy, with the oil market serving as the driving force in the Middle East and the success of newly industrialized countries (NICs) in Pacific Asia.

Concentration of the banking sector

Clearly, then, the structure of the banking sector has undergone profound changes in terms of the geographical redistribution of its hierarchy. We need now to look at the impact this change has had in terms of concentration.

A quick glance at the distribution of assets among the banks reveals no increase in concentration. If, in fact, there has been a transfer of power from the major banks in the United States to those in Japan, there is no indication that the power of the ten leading banks is any greater. Nor does a comparison of the proportion accounted for by the ten leading banks of the assets of the top twenty, 100 or 300 banks in 1974 and 1988 show any major alteration. The figures are respectively 60.6 percent, 23 percent, and 17.0 percent for 1974; and 60.2 percent, 25.6 percent, and 18.3 percent for 1988. There is, indeed, no need to calculate several concentration indices to come to the conclusion that in terms of concentration the structure of the world banking system has remained what it was fourteen years ago. Calculation of the relative value of the total activity of the ten and twenty leading world banks in relation to the activity of the top 100, or the total activity of the ten, twenty and 100 leading banks in relation to that of the top 300, reveals a certain stability. The ten leading banks accounted for 23 percent of the activity of the top 100 banks and 17 percent of the top 300 in 1974; these figures stood at 26 per cent and 20 percent in 1988. This relative stability is the same for the top twenty, which accounted for 38 percent of the activity of the top 100 in 1974 and 42 percent in 1987, and 28 percent of the activity of the top

TABLE 5.4 Increasing concentration of the world banking sector

	Total worth of banks ($bn)				*As % of total of top 100 banks*		*As % of total of top 300 banks*		
	Top 10	*Top 20*	*Top 100*	*Top 300*	*Top 10*	*Top 20*	*Top 10*	*Top 20*	*Top 100*
1974	377	622	1,629	2,223	23·15	38·15	16·9	27·9	73·8
1981	959	1,662	4,377	6,019	21·91	37·97	15·9	27·6	72·7
1985	1,331	2,280	5,943	3,251	22·39	38·37	14·4	24·0	64·2
1987	2,209	3,793	9,602	13,480	23·00	39·51	16·4	28·1	71·2
1988	2,767	4,597	10,829	13,641	25·55	42·45	18·3	30·4	71·6

Source: *The Banker*, Top 500, 1974, 1988, 1989.

300 in 1974 and 34 percent in 1987. As for the world's 100 leading banks, the importance of their activity remained unchanged, representing approximately 75 percent of that of the top 300.

This leads to the unexpected observation that the world banking sector has undergone *no fundamental change in the past fifteen years*. Its degree of concentration has remained comparable, despite an increase in the relative size of the top twenty between 1987 and 1988 (6 percent up in relation to the top 300 and 4 percent up in relation to the top 100). The world's ten leading banks represent approximately 17 percent of the sector as a whole (0.23 × 0.73); the top twenty, approximately 27 percent; and the top 300, approximately 70 percent. The fundamental transformation that would have occurred with a move from monopolistic competition to oligopoly did not take place.

However, we can identify two different forms of banking sector concentration that may occur in the future.

In the first case, that of external growth, the American banks – in particular the banks specializing in real estate, oil, and agriculture – as well as those with heavy exposure to the Third World, are almost forced by the nature of their commitments in developing countries to unite in order to reduce their handicaps and to position themselves within an economy which has debts with the rest of the world.

The second form of concentration is developing with the creation of the European single market. In response to the demands of their new environment and the removal of national limits or protections, European banks will need to consider over time a policy of mergers or absorptions at the request of their customers. It is, of course, still too early to determine what the future European banking hierarchy will be, but it is likely that the largest units will attempt to extend their networks by uniting with regional banks, while the small and medium-sized banks will be oriented toward the creation of a European network in association with institutions which will have the same professional criteria as their own. It is the logic of a new frontier to be expanded and a territory to be conquered that will influence how Europe's banking structure evolves. There will be difficulties. The announcement in September 1989 that Amro and the Générale de Banque were abandoning their plans to merge illustrates the difficulty of trying to bring together large banking networks from different countries on equal footing. The absence of a uniform fiscal and legal status (companies operating under European law), differences in culture, and insufficient attention to the implementation process explain to a large extent why this project failed.

With their activities increasingly internationalized and especially with the existence of instantaneous financial information transmission systems, large banks must react to the need for results in what is now a context of heightened competition. This is why banks such as Citicorp or the Sumitomo Bank are resolutely determined to become, and remain, global players. Their strategy is dominated by their will to achieve significant market penetration, first and foremost in their home territory and then in the other two regions. Citicorp aims to cover all the banking segments in all the principal industrial countries. In trading activities, it is present on the major stock exchanges in the United States, in Europe, in Tokyo, and in other Asian countries. The Sumitomo Bank, a member of the Japanese government bonds syndicate, has London branch offices specializing in the Euromarkets and is consolidating its drive toward greater involvement in securities trading in Europe and the United States. Excluded from capital markets (with the exception of Euromarkets and Japanese state bonds trading) by Japanese regulations, Sumitomo has transferred its activities from Tokyo to its London office. Its objective is clear: it wants to become the number one bank in the world in terms of assets and market share, and thus, ultimately, profitability. In order to achieve this goal, the bank, while maintaining the criterion of profitability at a satisfactory level, must strive to achieve a growing volume of activity. The bank's expansionist policy, moreover, is geared toward finding ways of circumventing legislative restrictions and performing indirectly a service which it cannot yet perform for its customers in Japan.

A NEW INTERNATIONAL HIERARCHY

Since 1970, the evolution of the banking structure has been marked by three main tendencies:

- the decline of the American banks;
- the rise in power of the Japanese banks;
- the stable position of the European banks.

The decline of American banks

The year 1974 will remain imprinted on the memory of American bankers: not as the point when the American banking system imploded with regard to the world system, but without doubt the year when American banks were toppled from world dominance. The Bank of America, the Chase Manhattan Bank, and Citicorp were for the last time the leading trio in world banking. Since then, the descent to the abyss has been only too familiar to the Bank of America – the institution which had dominated world banking throughout the 1970s (see table 5.5). In the span of five years, from 1983 to 1988, it plunged from second to forty-first position. Its assets decreased on average by 11 percent per year between 1985 and 1987. However, in 1988 the bank registered a 2.5 percent increase, suggesting that the end of the tunnel may be near. The organization's restructuring from its head office in San Francisco, California has led to the closure of one of its European offices in Edinburgh, Scotland. The Bank of America's ambition to remain in first place with a policy of rapid internationalization turned out a failure because of fundamental mistakes made in the selection of its senior management team and strategic priorities.

The case of the Chase Manhattan Bank is similar. However, its decline had already begun in 1975; ranking thirty-third in 1987, its fall was less abrupt than that of the Bank of America.

The only one of these three banks to remain in the top ten up to 1987 was Citicorp, with its global banking strategy. It has managed to increase its assets to a level above that of the American banking sector as a whole. Citicorp has enough

TABLE 5.5 Change in world ranking of the Bank of America, 1969–1988

Year	*Rank*
1969–78	1
1979	2
1980	2
1981	1
1982	2
1983	2
1984	4
1985	9
1986	24
1987	38
1988	41

Source: *The Banker*, Top 500, 1974–88.

going for it to maintain a pre-eminent position for a long period of time. Its thrust in consumer banking on a global scale (although predominantly in the US) and policy of investing in computerization of its financial services is in many respects unique. In the early 1970s, before the other banks felt the need, Citicorp was already equipping itself with an integrated computer system which modified all its service provisions. The revolutionary design of its system, based on interactive technology, enables the customer to enter the bank's database directly from his or her terminal. This technique, which gave individuals the opportunity to perform extremely complex operations at minimum cost, reduced processes as well as handling costs for information. It was in stark contrast to the predominant model of the time, characterized by multiple access points and therefore by a multitude of architectures and systems. In 1973, ITT commercialized point-of-sale terminals for Citibank. Today, there are more than 800 of these automatic teller machines (ATMs) in New York alone. This system, known as the consumer banking system (CBS), allows individuals to consult their accounts and to manage most of their relations with the bank.

In an attempt to strengthen its leading position in electronics and data processing, Citicorp entrusted one of its California branches specialized in computer processing with developing its software and studying the organizational functions as well as the financial aspects of its information-processing policy. Citicorp has devoted considerable financial resources to computerizing its customer services, spending close on $6 bn over a period of approximately eight years. The money has, for the most part, gone to the sectors of personal banking, money-market banking, and wholesale banking ($1.5 bn). In 1986, computer expenditure exceeded $0.5 bn of which $100 m were allocated to research and development. Citicorp's investments in information technology exceed the equity of all American financial holdings bar two. Citicorp has therefore acquired a lasting edge over its competitors.

Since 1979, Citicorp has also relentlessly extended the geographical reach of its computer system and has taken the option of a globally integrated system. It is also worth noting that the architecture adopted by Citicorp enables it to identify the computer system's capacity, its degree of utilization, and its profitability: all this, thanks to a modular approach.

The importance of Citicorp's commitment to data processing and computing is reflected in the number of people it employs. The institutional bank, which operates throughout the world, has nearly 2,000 technicians solely devoted to ensuring the system's proper functioning. Quality controls are now carried out in over fifty technical centers set up in thirty countries. The institutional bank's electronic network handles over 12,000 customers and over 17,000 products sold in 108 countries.

On the American market, Citicorp has enlarged the range of products it offers to individual customers. In view of the insufficient profitability of traditional deposit collection, Citicorp has built an electronics system covering the entire United States and a few foreign markets enabling it to compete with American regional banks on their own territory. Internally, there is also the computer system FOCUS which handles on a single account check transactions, market operations, Visa cards, and credit operations.

However, Citicorp's pre-eminence is not invulnerable in the long term. Indeed, it does not favor loyalty to commercial customers or its executives. Over the past four years, Citicorp's commercial bank and merchant bank teams in Europe and Asia have experienced a considerable turnover. So while its technological advance may enable it to maintain, or even increase, its market share in personal banking and in financial products and services, its position will be increasingly contested by other institutions such as the Deutsche Bank, the Union des Banques Suisses, the Banque Nationale de Paris, or the Société Générale, which also intend to favor industrial customer relations while simultaneously developing advanced technology products that may eventually match those that Citicorp already boasts.

The rapid disappearance of American banks from the leading ranks of bank classification based on assets is pinpointed by two revealing figures.

In 1974, they owned 41 percent of the total assets of the ten leading banks; in 1987, Citicorp, the sole representative of the United States in this closed circle, had no more than 8.98 percent; and American banks had the slowest assets growth rate. From 1974 to 1987, it stood at 2.65 percent – lower than that of Latin American banks (3.10 percent).

In 1988, even Citicorp fell out of the world's top ten, relegated to eleventh place by the entry into the top ten of two Japanese concerns, the Tokai Bank and the Mitsubishi Trust & Banking Corporation.

The rise to power of Japanese banks

In the space of fourteen years (1974–88) the number of Japanese banks present among the world's leading ten rose from three to six. The Dai Ichi Kangyo Bank was the first to join the top ten; it is now the world's number one bank in terms of assets. In 1974, the Japanese banking sector acounted for only 8 percent of the top ten's assets. In 1988 it had 92.25 percent. A comparison of these two figures to the evolution of American banks immediately reveals that the Japanese banks did more than just take the place of the American banks; they ousted the British

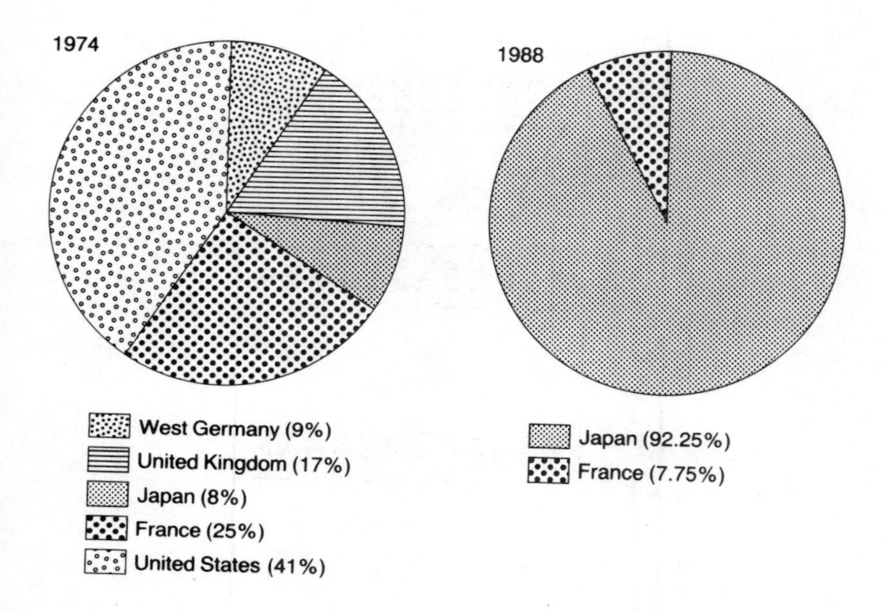

FIGURE 5.2 Geographical distribution of the assets of the top 10 banks, 1974 and 1988
Source: *The Banker*

banks and the Deutsche Bank out of this classification completely and reduced the French bank presence from three to one.

This unprecedented drive to accumulate assets was made possible on the one hand by the investments and acquisitions of the Dai Ichi Kangyo Bank and, on the other hand, by the emergence of new banks such as Fuji, Sumitomo, Mitsubishi, and Sanwa. The arrival of these banks among the top ten was quite exceptional considering their initial low ranking. Over the period under examination the Fuji Bank rose from thirteenth to third place, the Mitsubishi Bank from twelfth to fourth, Sumitomo from tenth to second and Sanwa from fifteenth to fifth.

On 1 April 1990 the Mitsui and Taiyo Kobe Banks merged. This union of the two institutions which, prior to the merger, were Japan's seventh and eighth most important commercial banks, makes them the world's second largest bank group. The

TABLE 5.6 The world's leading banks in 1988 (in terms of assets held)

Rank	*Bank*	*Country*	*Assets 1988*[a] *($m)*	*Change 1987–8 (%)*	*Net income 1988*[a] *($m)*	*Change 1987–8(%)*
1	Dai Ichi Kangyo	Japan	383,767·8	−10·4	1,360·1	+28·0
2	Sumitomo	Japan	368,981·8	−13·6	1,500·0	+69·2
3	Fuji	Japan	354,026·5	−12·2	1,301·1	+27·5
4	Mitsubishi	Japan	246,169·4	−11·1	1,266·3	+31·2
5	Sanwa	Japan	338,399·4	+12·8	1,176·2	+28·8
6	Industrial Bank of Japan	Japan	259,509·1	+ 8·0	707·3	+18·7
7	Norinchukin	Japan	243,761·7	+ 5·2	308·6	+12·5
8	Tokai	Japan	222,879·7	+ 6·2	455·4	+14·0
9	Crédit agricole	France	210,595·8	− 2·8	643·7	+39·8
10	Citicorp	United States	207,666·0	− 2·0	1,858·0	–
11	Mitsui	Japan	205,053·7	+ 5·9	600·6	+23·7
12	Taiyo Kobe	Japan	174,972·8	+ 5·0	404·7	+22·9

[a] Fiscal year 1988.
Source: ICBA Banking Analysis.

TABLE 5.7 Assets of the seven leading Japanese banks[a] as proportion of total assets of the world top 10, 20, 100, and 300 banks

Assets of the seven banks	*1974*	*1981*	*1985*	*1987*	*1988*
Total, in $bn	147	496	901	1,513	2,133
as % of top 10	38·85	51·75	67·69	73·04	77·09
as % of top 20	23·57	29·94	39·50	42·53	46·41
as % of top 100	8·99	11·33	15·16	16·80	19·70
as % of top 300	6·50	3·24	9·74	11·97	14·10

[a] Dai Ichi Kangyo, Sumitomo, Fuji, Mitsubishi, Sanwa, Industrial Bank of Japan, Norinchukin.
Source: *The Banker*, 1975, 1982, 1986, 1988.

merger brought into being a network of some 590 branches in Japan (against 354 for Dai Ichi Kangyo) and over twenty-five foreign offices. An unprecedented move since the formation of the Taiyo Kobe Bank itself in 1973, this operation is undoubtedly the most spectacular result of the deregulation and internationalization of Japan's financial system, made possible largely by the voluntary and decisive intervention of Japan's Ministry of Finance (MOF). The effectiveness of this new institution should be closely observed, for the merging of two basically different corporate cultures in Japanese banking may well not be easy.

The internationalization of Japan's banks seems to have reached maturity. The growth in assets of its seven leading banks is well above that of the 300 leading banks. Between 1974 and 1988, their assets underwent a 14½-fold increase in value and 80 percent of them increased their relative weight in banking assets (based on the top 10, 20, 100, and 300 banks). Likewise, the market share of these banks on Euromarkets has reached such a level so quickly that voices are heard from time to time accusing the Japanese banks of dumping and "buying market share" by offering loans to corporations at significantly lower rates than their European and American competitors. Such a rapid growth in international activities may come as a surprise, considering the importance they attribute to relationships when choosing financial partners. In fact they have rapidly penetrated foreign financial markets by applying the so-called commercial targets technique. Mobilizing all their resources to create a volume effect, they have successively conquered the debt market and the Eurobond market and are now turning their attention toward the mergers and acquisition and project financing markets.

Sumitomo has a sizeable set-up in the United States, with some fifty branches in California, and an international network including subsidiaries in London, Switzerland, Bahrain, and Hong Kong, all active in the Eurobond market. Another bank that deserves to be mentioned is the oldest international Japanese bank, the Bank of Tokyo, which from the time of its foundation in 1946 asserted its international vocation; heir to the Yokohama Specie Bank, founded in 1880, its creation marked the beginning of Japanese international banking. This historical background explains the density of the Bank of Tokyo's foreign branch network, compared with other Japanese banks.

The strategy of the long-term credit banks is representative of Japan's desire to take advantage of opportunities abroad. Underlying their move was the opportunity offered them to export their experience in the area of long-term financing to foreign countries and institutions. Their first target was the Eurobond market, where only Nomura Securities and Daiwa Securities outranked the Industrial Bank of Japan and the Long Term Credit Bank in Eurobond subscriptions managed by Japanese financial institutions. Of the three principal institutions – Long Term Credit Bank, Nippon Credit Bank, and the Industrial Bank of Japan – the last is unquestionably the best placed in terms of international ambitions, financial power, and the outstanding quality of its teams. The Long Term Credit Bank is also rapidly becoming a global player: within just a few years it has won international recognition for its industrial expertise and its know-how in mergers and acquisitions. With some $18 bn worth of hidden reserves in January 1990 (largely made up of minority equity holdings in a broad spectrum of companies) they have the financial resources, the research capabilities, and the breadth of customer base to become a significant player on the world banking scene.

This new Japanese supremacy is especially startling since it both materialized very rapidly and seems to rest on very solid foundations. A look at the past of these banks reveals that their rise in the ranks did not actually begin until after 1980. Some of them, not yet among the top ten but among the top twenty, have taken just as commendable a route, considering the fact that in 1969, for example, Mitsubishi Trust & Banking and Sumitomo Trust & Banking were in 162nd and 189th position respectively. The Mitsubishi group has seen both its deposit bank and its merchant bank appear in the top ten; and Sumitomo had climbed to fifteenth position by 1988. These two banks saw their assets grow at the rate of 24.2 percent and 17.6 percent respectively in 1987 alone.

The early 1990s may well see a period of real domination of the banking sector by Japan, and one that will endure for some time.

European banks: Maintaining their position?

The idea that Europe's banks are maintaining their position is more a case of wishful thinking in Europe than actual fact. Of the six European banks (three French, two British, and one German) present in the top ten in 1974, only one was still there in 1987. Their share in total assets of the ten leading banks fell during the same period from 53 percent to 7.75 percent. A real decline in European banking has therefore occurred, purely to the advantage of the Japanese banks.

A closer look at how the classification of European banks (including British banks) has evolved reveals that they were the first to benefit from the decline of American banks; the high point of this trend came in 1979 when Crédit Agricole ranked number one. In a way, it can be said that they stood in for the Japanese banks until the latter reached a degree of maturity sufficient to take the place of the American banks.

Closer examination of the European banking sector reveals that the French banks stood their ground with assets growing twice as fast (8.02 percent) as those of English banks and three times quicker than those of American banks. The same can be said of the evolution of the European banking sector on a country basis with regard to the top twenty or 300 banks. The French, Swiss, and Italian banks have maintained their positions, while the West German banks have improved theirs and the British and American banks have gone on a downward trend.

For the French banks, the period 1974 to 1987 was one of high stability. The effort to accumulate assets was mainly the work of the large French banks: Banque Nationale de Paris, Crédit Agricole, and Crédit Lyonnais. Their assets all increased at least threefold. Crédit Agricole, which was not one of the top ten in 1974, ranked eighth in 1988. Moreover, Crédit Agricole's evolution was one of the most curious during this period. In 1975, it suddenly soared in the classification up to third place, where it remained until moving up a notch to second in 1978 and then to first place in 1979. After that the road was downhill, falling in one year's time (1981–2) from fourth to tenth position before resuming an upward slope and inching its way back to ninth position in 1986 and eighth in 1988. BNP fell from fourth place in 1974 to twelfth in 1988, confirming its stability over the past sixteen years (1973–88), a period during which it has oscillated between twelfth and fourth places. This stability, too, was achieved through an effort to accumulate assets, with a fourfold increase between 1974 and 1985. A notable development in France during this period was the departure of the Société Générale from the top ten. After much sustained effort, which led it from thirty-fourth place in 1970 to thirteenth in 1973, it maintained a strong position in the top ten until 1983, when it began a downward path to eleventh, fourteenth, twentieth, and nineteenth positions in 1984, 1985, 1986, and 1987.

Globally, the number of French banks included among the top twenty has remained constant over sixteen years at three, even if the relative importance of these three banks has diminished compared with the seventeen other leading banks.

In 1974, two British banks (Barclays and National Westminster) ranked among the top ten, accounting for 17 percent of their combined assets. In 1986, both had gone. Barclays made its exit between 1977 and 1979, but returned to its number nine position in 1980 before disappearing again in 1985.

National Westminster left the top ten a year earlier in 1984 and is now in seventeenth place, after less prosperous times between 1977 and 1979 when it left the top twenty, having for a long time previously (1970–6) been among the top ten. There are many factors contributing to the decline in the British presence in top ranks of banking, of which the degree of industrialization and the quality of the strategic choices made in the United Kingdom, in particular those concerning people and decision-making processes, are perhaps the most important.

The same fate – total banishment from the top ten – awaits West Germany. Only the Deutsche Bank was still present in 1977, with excellent results, but it disappeared in 1983. Since that time it has recovered and in 1987 the bank ranked eleventh in the world. In 1988–9 it underwent unprecedented structural reform based on specialization and vertical segmentation (by customers and products) in preference to the universal approach carried out at regional level. This implies some loss of autonomy by the large regional offices in favor of the head office, particularly in the areas of retail and investment banking. Indeed, the complexity of structures has to be alleviated by eliminating co-ordinating functions.

The Deutsche Bank still remains very much a domestic bank, with 62 percent of its volume of business and 83 percent of its gross profit coming from the domestic market. Nevertheless, since 1984, it has been conducting a very active strategy to become the leading European bank, in particular buying into foreign banking institutions. Today it continues to consolidate and diversify its position, with 191 international subsidiaries or branch offices under its control. These, however, only generate 17 percent of the bank's gross profit (13 percent Europe, 2 percent United States, 2 percent Asia, Latin America, and Australia). The transformation of the Deutsche Bank into a truly global institution remains a challenge, because it is still underrepresented on the two most important capital markets, the United States and Japan.

Its more recent priority is to become the leading banking institution in East Germany, where it can play a decisive role in the modernization of Germany's eastern provinces, as well as to become the premier universal bank in the European Community and offering a selected range of products and services in the United States and the Pacific region. It is particularly active throughout Europe.[1] In Austria, it has announced plans to take over Antoni, Hacker and Company, a small private bank giving access to the Austrian securities market; in the United Kingdom it was the third largest subscriber of Eurobonds in 1988 and as of the beginning of 1990 owns the London merchant bank Morgan Grenfell; it purchased the Italian operations of Bank of America in 1986, thus acquiring 100 branch offices with $3.1 bn in assets. In Portugal it took full control of MDM Sociedade de Investimento SA, an investment bank in Lisbon and in early 1989 acquired a majority investment in the Banco Comercial Transatlantico, a middle-market Spanish bank. And in 1988 it took full control of the Amsterdam bank H. Albert de Bary and Company.

New configuration

We can see, then, that the change in the world's banking structures has been marked by the gradual disappearance from the leading ranks of British and West German banks (the Deutsche Bank apart) and by the emergence of Japanese and, to a lesser extent, French banks, with the well-established banks consolidating their position and in some cases (especially the Japanese institutions) joining the top ten. Efforts toward concentration and the formation of new oligopolies have been the determining factors in the evolution of Japanese banking.

The evaluation of banks' total assets conceals the diversity of the changes which have affected their destiny and which can be better assessed on the basis of their market value. Using market capitalization[2] as the assessment criterion gets round certain shortcomings inherent in other criteria, because stock market prices, which at all times reflect information available on the company, remain over a long period of time one of the best estimates of a firm's worth.

According to the criterion of market capitalization, there is a relative decline in the United States and stagnation in Europe,

TABLE 5.8 Evolution of the 1988 world top 20 banks (in terms of assets), 1969–1988

Bank	*1969*	*1971*	*1973*	*1975*	*1977*	*1978*	*1981*	*1983*	*1984*	*1985*	*1986*	*1987*	*1988*
Dai Ichi Kangyo	–	5	5	10	11	10	9	3	2	2	1	1	1
Sumitomo Bank	17	19	10	15	15	14	11	5	5	4	3	2	2
Fuji	13	15	8	13	14	14	13	4	3	3	2	3	3
Mitsubishi Bank	10	20	12	15	16	16	14	4	6	5	4	4	4
Sanwa	18	21	15	18	18	18	17	9	7	7	5	5	5
Industrial Bank of Japan	28	34	22	25	25	22	25	18	15	13	8	6	6
Norinchukin	–	–	–	–	27	19	20	17	13	11	7	9	7
Crédit Agricole	–	–	–	3	3	1	4	10	9	8	9	7	8
Tokai	36	40	25	33	33	35	27	22	17	17	11	16	9
Mitsubishi Trust & Banking	162	48	51	56	54	52	46	26	25	21	15	13	10
Citicorp	2	2	2	2	2	3	2	1	1	1	5	8	11
Banque Nationale de Paris	15	7	4	5	5	4	3	6	7	6	10	10	12
Mitsui	29	43	30	36	36	36	24	19	21	18	13	18	13
Barclays	4	4	6	9	14	9	6	8	12	16	18	14	14
Sumitomo Trust & Banking	189	52	45	62	57	57	55	35	30	22	16	17	15
Crédit Lyonnais	21	11	11	7	7	6	7	13	11	14	20	12	16
NatWest	7	6	7	11	17	11	10	12	14	12	17	15	17
Bank of Tokyo	26	46	34	28	32	43	22	21	22	24	22	22	18
Deutsche Bank	24	8	9	6	4	5	9	14	18	15	14	11	19
Taiyo Kobe	–	–	33	38	43	42	37	32	27	26	27	21	20

Source: The Banker, Top 500, 1970–89.

TABLE 5.9 The fate of the 1969 world top 20 banks, to 1988

Bank	*1969*	*1971*	*1973*	*1975*	*1977*	*1979*	*1981*	*1983*	*1984*	*1985*	*1986*	*1987*	*1988*
Bank of America	1	1	1	1	1	2	1	2	4	9	24	38	41
Citicorp	2	2	2	2	2	3	2	1	1	1	6	8	11
Chase Manhattan	3	3	3	4	6	12	15	16	16	19	30	33	39
Barclays	4	4	6	9	12	9	6	8	12	16	18	14	14
Manufacturers Hanover	5	10	18	16	20	24	21	23	19	27	40	58	66
J. P. Morgan	6	12	17	19	22	29	30	29	26	31	38	54	43
National Westminster	7	6	7	11	17	11	10	12	14	12	17	15	17
First Interstate Bank	8	13	27	39	50	60	54	44	45	53	61	81	75
Banca Nazionale del Lavoro	9	9	14	20	26	23	41	45	42	39	41	35	44
Chemical New York	10	17	23	23	24	40	44	40	37	43	56	50	63
Bankers Trust	11	26	26	32	48	55	60	56	47	52	66	76	80
Royal Bank of Canada	12	18	28	22	23	34	16	20	24	32	45	57	50
Fuji Bank	13	15	8	13	14	14	13	4	3	3	2	3	3
Westdeutschland Bank	14	14	20	21	13	13	23	37	43	38	36	34	38
Banque Nationale de Paris	15	7	4	5	5	4	3	6	7	6	10	10	12
Mitsubishi	16	10	12	17	16	17	14	7	6	5	4	4	4
Sumitomo	17	19	10	15	15	16	13	5	5	4	3	2	2
Sanwa	18	21	15	18	18	18	17	9	7	7	5	5	5
CIBC (Canada)	19	25	35	29	30	41	31	34	38	46	63	68	61
Midland	20	23	21	27	42	26	12	15	20	20	34	39	37

Source: *The Banker*, Top 500, 1970–89.

despite very moderate growth for a few banks such as the Deutsche Bank, NatWest, and Barclays. Meanwhile, observers have noted an upward movement in Japan illustrated especially vividly by Sumitomo's lightning advance, and the rapid and relentless evolution of Dai Ichi Kangyo and of Industrial Bank of Japan. Following at a slower but still very strong pace are banks like Fuji and Sanwa.

Until 1980 there was no great difference between the growth rates of market capitalizations of European and Japanese banks – even a slight discrepancy in favor of the European banks. The Deutsche Bank provides a clear illustration of this: in 1975 it had a 74 percent growth rate (from $1,184 m to $2,063 m) while the Industrial Bank of Japan was at 16 percent and Sumitomo's market capitalization fell by 0.16 percent. And in 1980 Barclays, with a 36 percent growth rate, was ahead of the best-performing Japanese bank, the Industrial Bank of Japan, with

TABLE 5.10 Rank of non-American banks with capitalization of over $2 bn

	1980	*1981*	*1982*	*1983*	*1984*	*1985*
Barclays	10	14	11	13	17	13
Dai Ichi Kangyo	3	1	1	1	2	2
Deutsche Bank	9	8	9	7	10	10
Fuji	5	5	3	2	3	3
Industrial Bank of Japan	13	7	7	6	8	6
Mitsubishi Bank	4	3	4	3	5	4
NatWest	12	3	4	14	5	17
Sanwa	5	4	2	4	4	5
Sumitomo	5	2	5	5	1	1

Source: International Capital Perspective, Geneva.

TABLE 5.11 Evolution of a few representative banks in terms of market capitalization ($m)

Bank	*1973*	*1974*	*1975*	*1978*	*1980*	*1981*	*1983*	*1984*	*1985*
Barclays	1,931	1,479	–	1,608	3,212	2,027	2,218	2,127	4,795
Deutsche Bank	1,361	1,184	2,063	3,687	3,253	2,791	3,259	3,461	7,499
Industrial Bank of Japan	1,746	1,077	1,253	2,413	2,313	2,906	3,552	5,340	11,342
Sumitomo	2,870	2,051	1,704	2,787	3,498	3,783	4,770	11,201	17,703

35 percent. However, by 1983 the Japanese banks had begun to overtake the others. In 1984 and 1985, the Industrial Bank of Japan was at 50 percent and 112 percent respectively, and Sumitomo at 134 percent and 58 percent; Barclays' and the Deutsche Bank's average annual growth rate of 50 percent was attributable solely to their slight advance in fiscal year 1983–4. Japanese domination, visible in terms of growth rate, becomes even more apparent in terms of absolute value of capitalizations: $17,703 m for Sumitomo in 1985, $11,342 m for the Industrial Bank of Japan, against $7,332 m for Citicorp, $7,499 m for the Deutsche Bank, and a mere $4,005 m for Barclays.

Just as startling is Japanese preponderance among banks with market capitalization in excess of $1,000 m and $2,000 m. In 1973, thirty-one Japanese banks and forty European institutions had capitalizations of over $1,000 m; in 1975, these figures had changed to twenty-six for Japan and forty-three for Europe. In 1980 the numbers of Japanese and European banks with capitalizations over $2,000 m were twenty-five and thirty-five respectively; in 1983, forty-five and thirty-eight, with Japan gaining supremacy for the first time; in 1985, eighty-two and sixty-nine, with Japan consolidating its leading position.

Individually, banks have not always been ranked by total assets. Leading American banks, like Citicorp, have lower capitalizations than would appear from their total assets. During the period 1974–86, Citicorp's market value increased at a rate of 1.17 percent. Such a growth rate could have been explained by a strong market capitalization of $3,371 m in 1974, i.e., the combined total capitalization of NatWest ($541 m), Barclays ($631 m), Midland ($317 m), Manufacturers Hanover ($787 m), and Deutsche Bank ($1,355 m) or even the sum of the consolidated capitalization of Sumitomo, Dai Ichi Kangyo, and Daiwa. This shift in the balance of power in 1986 is startling. Citicorp's market capitalization was a mere $7,332 m, compared with Sumitomo's $34,476 m, the Industrial Bank of Japan's $30,888 m, and Dai Ichi Kangyo's $29,952 m. Even the Daiwa Bank, which is the smallest of Japan's world-oriented banks, had a market capitalization of $9,516 m in 1986, therefore also outranking Citicorp.

It should be underlined that the Japanese banks' market capitalization grew more rapidly than their total assets, which indicates the quality of their strategies and of their implementation. The European banks, thanks to margins that they were able to retain, are in a situation where the valuation of their assets is a good indicator of their capitalization. This is the case for the Deutsche Bank, which from 1975 to 1982 had its most outstanding performances in terms of total assets and market capitalization, as a result of a fundamental strategic decision to make German industrial development the cornerstone of this institution's growth. In order to acquire a pre-eminent position and retain it, the bank undertook to further strengthen its top-level teams, to reorganize its decision-making process to make it more customer-sensitive, and to allocate its capital and human resources in support of its strategic priorities.

TABLE 5.12 Classification of Japanese and European banks in terms of market capitalization, 1975–1985

	No. of banks with market capitalization exceeding:				
Region/country	*$1,000m 1975*	*$1,500m 1978*	*$2,000m 1980*	*$2,000m 1983*	*$2,000m 1985*
Japan	26	40	25	45	82
Europe	43	35	35	38	69
United Kingdom	13	10	16	18	31
West Germany	10	13	8	10	18
France	3	1	2		2

The consistency of this policy, pursued since the beginning of the century, and the systematic assignment of the best talent to implement this strategy, explain why today the market value of the Deutsche Bank's industrial investments exceeds its market capitalization.

We may therefore conclude that the inequality between total assets and market capitalization is due, among other things, to the fact that the creation of assets in the form of loans and off-balance-sheet commitments represents a decreasing proportion of the banking business. On the other hand, the differential between stock market capitalization and the balance-sheet total of certain banks is an indication of considerable differences in current wealth and positionings, therefore of wealth to come. Two trends have favored the relative over-valuation of Japanese banks: first, the rise in real estate prices, the built square meter in Japan being around fifty times more expensive than in the United States; and secondly, the stock market performance of Japanese industrial companies, which has enabled banks owning often minority holdings in these companies' capital to accumulate considerable latent capital gains, part of which has been used during the past five years to equalize year-end profits. The low intrinsic profitability of the domestic market and the cost of foreign investment have put numerous Japanese banks in a situation where arbitrages of assets have made an often essential contribution to fiscal year profits.

It is worth noting that the total assets criterion gives no indication of the nature of these assets and consequently does not provide qualitative assessment. However, it should also be stressed that market capitalization has its imperfections too, in that the extent of day-to-day variations often depends on factors outside the firm, such as the world economic situation or the state of international financial markets. Considering the shortcomings of both criteria, it is appropriate to complete this analysis with an evaluation of net assets, defined and calculated in accounting terms as the sum of banks' shareholder equity, and provisions for general risks. This criterion also has its limits because of the heterogeneity of accounting practices, in particular with regard to provisions!

An analysis of the evolution of provisions for doubtful debts in the United States, the country with the highest bank failure rate, offers many lessons. At the end of 1986, First Interstate led American banks in this respect with provisions of $910 m, a 14.8 percent increase from 1985. Manufacturers Hanover Trust followed with $858.9 m (+37.9 percent from 1985); Chemical Bank had $668.7 m (+8.1 percent); Chase Manhattan, $595 m (+36.8 percent); and First Chicago, $585 m (+38.1 percent). Citicorp was back in ninth place with $463.3 m (+126.5 percent), indicating a policy of systematic under-provisioning. This situation had to be adjusted in 1987 when Citicorp was forced to build up more than $2 billion in reserves essentially on developing-country debts.

Examination of provisions and banks' shareholder equity for various countries reveals that American banks, often involved in very risky lending activities, have considerably reinforced their equity over the past ten years. On the other hand, the Japanese, for tax purposes, considering the quality of their commercial loans and the size of their latent reserves of securities and real estate, have a particularly low level of equity and provisions for doubtful debts. Europe's situation once again appears to be closer to that of the United States than to Japan's.

If it has become convenient to use shareholders' equity as a criterion of evaluation, it is precisely because it expresses the most familiar financial risk to practitioners of finance, even if the theoretical work of Modigliani and Miller placed less emphasis on the negative psychological impact of debt in total liabilities. These imperfections in accounting for equity and provisions have led to the adoption of other criteria of evaluation, such as profits and productivity indices. However, these criteria also have their limits, because over a short period of time they only imperfectly reflect a bank's profit-making capacity.

The allocation of overhead to more or less profitable sectors, the intrinsic quality of assets, the bank's practice with regard to provisions on commitments or evaluating different elements of worth, are all factors which vary from one bank to the next. Therefore, whatever conclusions may be drawn must be interpreted with caution as they can differ from those obtained according to other criteria.

In 1985, for example, the Nippon Credit Bank had profits before taxes of $94,400 per employee; the Long Term Credit Bank, $84,000; the Industrial Bank of Japan, $69,083; Sumitomo Bank, $52,385; the Fuji Bank, $43,800; and the Dai Ichi Kangyo Bank, $30,400; whereas Citicorp's pre-tax profits were $21,000 per employee, followed by the Société Générale at $19,000, Chase Manhattan at $19,000, the Dresdner Bank at $11,000, BNP at $8,400 and Paribas at $6,800. It is worth noting that

TABLE 5.13 Capital/assets ratios, 1981–1988 (%)

Bank	*1981*	*1982*	*1983*	*1984*	*1985*	*1986*	*1987*	*1988*
Banque Nationale de Paris	1·28	1·34	1·53	1·51	1·98	3·15	3·17	2·83
Banque Bruxelles Lambert	1·81	1·49	1·68	1·55	1·61	2·10	2·04	2·10
Dresdner Bank	2·93	2·88	2·68	2·66	2·82	3·24	3·23	3·30
Allgemeine Bank	2·37	2·52	2·75	2·67	2·91	3·51	3·96	3·68
Deutsche Bank	3·10	3·27	3·24	3·33	3·99	3·93	4·06	3·78
Banca Nazionale del Lavoro	3·85	3·84	2·88	4·11	4·70	5·39	3·80	3·80
Barclays	4·66	4·68	4·56	3·53	5·07	4·71	4·83	5·57
Union des Banques Suisses	5·67	5·14	4·97	5·09	5·78	5·71	6·08	6·10
Citicorp	3·80	3·98	4·58	4·50	4·64	4·73	4·33	4·84
Bank of America	3·54	3·97	4·45	4·50	3·96	3·39	3·59	4·45
Chase Manhattan	4·77	4·26	4·75	4·93	5·25	5·37	3·31	4·34
Sumitomo	3·13	2·95	2·96	2·25	2·85	2·95	2·20	2·55
Dai Ichi Kangyo	3·26	2·86	2·63	2·51	2·38	2·38	1·79	2·75
Fuji	3·51	3·00	2·98	2·82	2·82	2·89	2·20	2·75
Arithmetic average	3·41	3·30	3·33	3·28	3·63	3·82	3·19	3·68

Source: *The Banker*, 1983–9.

TABLE 5.14 Ratio of pretax profits to assets, 1981–1987

Bank	*1981*	*1982*	*1983*	*1984*	*1985*	*1986*	*1987*
Banque National de Paris	0·42	0·36	0·35	0·35	0·40	0·54	0·48
Banque Bruxelles Lambert	0·58	0·24	0·26	0·25	0·25	0·35	0·47
Allgemeine Bank	0·44	0·43	0·53	0·45	0·51	0·54	0·49
Dresdner Bank	0·32	0·38	0·50	0·53	0·53	0·55	0·49
Banca Nazionale del Lavoro	0·31	0·31	0·25	0·38	0·52	0·52	0·23
Barclays	1·32	0·91	0·90	0·95	1·29	1·24	0·41
Deutsche Bank	0·68	0·67	0·93	0·87	1·09	1·10	1·10
Union des Banques Suisses	0·71	0·69	0·71	0·73	0·77	0·78	0·70
Bank of America	0·59	0·44	0·44	0·40	−0·37	−0·32	−0·90
Citicorp	0·74	1·11	1·30	1·15	1·11	0·95	−0·12
Chase Manhattan	0·77	0·50	0·92	0·80	1·08	0·95	−0·74
Sumitomo	0·46	0·59	0·78	0·61	0·58	0·63	0·37
Dai Ichi Kangyo	0·35	0·39	0·45	0·48	0·44	0·43	0·54
Fuji	0·44	0·63	0·55	0·65	0·51	0·53	0·63
Arithmetic average	0·58	0·55	0·64	0·61	0·62	0·63	0·30

Source: The Banker, 1983–8.

these figures were particularly significant in 1985, whereas they were less convincing in 1987, on account of reserves built up in the United States and in Europe for risks on developing countries.

The per-employee earnings of the world's leading banks confirm the net advance of Japan, the decline of the United States, and the intermediate position of Europe – a general view which conceals many discrepancies.

TABLE 5.15 Equity/assets ratio, 1983–1988 (%)

	1983	*1984*	*1985*	*1986*	*1987*	*1988*
Japanese banks						
Arithmetic average	1·73	2·29	2·35	2·40	1·91	2·33
Dai Ichi Kangyo	2·63	2·51	2·38	2·38	1·79	2·41
Sumitomo Bank	2·96	2·25	2·85	2·95	2·20	2·55
Fuji	2·98	2·83	2·82	2·89	2·20	2·75
Mitsubishi Bank	2·83	2·85	2·88	2·99	2·14	2·58
Sanwa	2·78	2·67	2·70	2·61	1·96	2·46
Industrial Bank of Japan	2·33	2·38	2·84	2·80	2·43	3·12
Norinchukin Bank	0·46	0·50	0·47	0·47	0·52	0·55
Mitsubishi Trust & Banking	0·23	2·18	2·06	2·22	2·34	3·08
Tokai	0·45	2·51	2·65	2·60	1·62	2·38
Sumitomo Trust & Banking	0·28	2·34	2·15	2·29	1·43	1·80
Mitsui	2·41	2·43	2·36	2·52	1·88	1·32
Long-Term Credit Bank of Japan	0·47	2·08	2·05	2·11	2·37	2·93
American banks						
Arithmetic average	4·59	4·64	4·62	4·48	3·74	4·54
Citicorp	4·58	4·50	4·64	4·73	4·33	4·84
Chase Manhattan	4·75	4·93	5·25	5·37	3·31	4·34
Bank of America	4·45	4·50	3·96	3·39	3·59	4·45
European banks						
Arithmetic average	3·33	2·68	3·23	3·79	4·19	4·27
Crédit Agricole	4·24	4·15	4·26	4·36	4·43	4·08
Banque nationale de Paris	1·53	1·51	1·98	3·15	3·17	2·83
Deutsche Bank	3·24	3·33	3·99	3·93	4·06	3·78
Crédit Lyonnais	–	1·14	1·23	1·91	2·64	3·02
Barclays	4·56	3·53	5·07	4·71	4·89	5·57
National Westminster	4·79	3·68	4·10	5·54	5·70	6·11
Société Générale	1·32	1·36	2·03	2·90	3·23	3·35
Midland	3·61	2·74	3·18	3·80	5·34	5·45
Arithmetic average	2·63	2·74	2·95	3·15	2·94	3·29

Source: *The Banker*, June 1984–July 1989.

TABLE 5.16 Ratio of equity total assets

Bank	*1987*	*Ratio 1*[a]	*Ratio 2*[b]
Dai Ichi Kangyo	1·79	2·87	9·66
Sumitomo	3·14	3·11	9·09
Fuji	2·72	3·31	9·70
Mitsubishi	2·65	3·22	11·89
Sanwa	2·05	3·02	9·86

[a] Including potential capital gains.
[b] Excluding potential capital gains.

TABLE 5.17 Profit per employee, ($ per capita)

Bank	*1983*	*1984*	*1985*	*1986*	*1987*	*% change 1987–8*
Japanese banks						
Dai Ichi Kangyo	20,260	24,539	30,432	49,488	70,902	3·50
Sumitomo Bank	54,505	40,524	52,395	89,249	51,627	0·95
Fuji	37,477	35,904	43,835	71,068	97,079	2·59
Mitsubishi Bank	24,607	34,073	40,601	73,166	101,855	4·14
Industrial Bank of Japan	75,560	73,564	69,053	163,010	145,614	1·93
Sanwa	27,756	29,001	38,552	62,060	81,257	2·93
Norinchukin Bank	33,374	–	48,470	64,313	74,547	2·23
Mitsubishi Trust & Banking	19,251	23,055	44,923	115,505	180,154	9·16
Tokai	19,031	22,027	26,596	39,681	54,249	2·85
Sumitomo Trust & Banking	22,449	26,812	49,757	122,395	169,264	7·54
Mitsui	26,533	22,811	28,852	58,688	90,158	3·39
Long-term Credit Bank of Japan	73,725	64,357	84,031	154,923	195,689	2·55
American banks						
Citicorp	25,212	21,746	21,107	19,209	−2,667	
Chase Manhattan	18,891	14,438	19,324	17,772	−16,938	
Bank of America	5,545	5,189	−5,334	−5,110	−14,613	
European banks						
Crédit Agricole	7,057			7,225	11,524	1·63
Banque nationale de Paris	5,510	5,397	8,440	13,173	14,577	2·65
Deutsche Bank	14,707	12,707	21,250	27,418	18,872	1·28
Crédit Lyonnais		6,740	7,945	11,523	15,778	
Barclays	6,569	6,017	11,648	11,993	6,345	0·97
National Westminster	7,935	8,623	12,623	15,859	12,918	1·63
Société Générale	4,347	4,576	8,473	14,287	15,446	3·55
Midland	3,947	1,937	6,451	9,476	−16,080	

Source: *The Banker*, June 1984–July 1988.

Profit per employee of the Japanese banks increased on average more than twofold (2.5 times), although in some cases there was a threefold increase and even a fourfold increase for the Mitsubishi Bank (4.14 times). The Dai Ichi Kangyo Bank's profit per employee increased by 3.5 and continues to rise steadily. From 1983 to 1987, profit per employee continued to grow: $20,260, $24,539, $30,432, $49,488, and $70,902.

In large American banks' profit-per-employee figure became negative in 1985, starting with the Bank of America (−$5,000) and then in 1987 with Citicorp (−$2,667), Chase Manhattan (−$16,938), and the Midland Bank (−$16,080). This reflects a downward trend, probably irreversible in the short term, that is due to a multitude of factors to do with strategy and corporate culture. Among these is the large amount of financial risk assumed on developing countries and in the framework of leveraged buy-out (LBO) financing. One of the most important financial indices for long-term measurement of the quality of a bank's management is the ratio of profit before taxes to total assets. Often less than 1, this ratio only rarely exceeds such a figure.

6

◇

The Factors behind the Evolution: The United States, Europe, and Japan

◆

It is not enough to describe a system in order to determine its evolution. Although the system has an influence on the future of its components, it is itself dependent on the forces inherent in each and every one of them. In the light of this, and taking into account the internationalization of financing and the move toward a united European banking community, it is essential that we determine the strengths and weaknesses of the three major banking centers. We will therefore examine banking in the United States, in Europe, and finally in Japan, in the knowledge that among the issues facing banks are commitments on developing countries, the implementation of the Cooke ratio, and profitability trends as an indicator of the quality of the strategic decisions made over the last twenty-five years.

THE AMERICAN BANKS

Falling profitability

In 1979, banking profits in the United States began a steady downward trend that lasted until 1985, when there was a slight recovery. In 1985, banks insured by the FDIC saw their profitability rate on assets reach its lowest level in fifteen years.

The same fluctuations occurred with the market rate of return.

In a global context of improving results, 1988 was marked by a return to net earnings of some $18.9 bn, compared with losses of $2.1 bn in 1987 and $13 bn in 1986 (figures concern the 200 leading banks in the United States). The same survey reveals that the ratio of net earnings to assets improved (0.83 percent in 1988 versus 0.6 percent in 1986), as did earnings per share (up 15.7 percent against 11.4 percent in 1986). This improvement in results did not, however, place America's leading banks in a very comfortable situation with regard to the demands of the Cooke ratio for 1992. In view of this deadline, analysts are attempting to determine the impact that readjustment will have on the banks when they bring themselves in step with international norms. Estimates of the capital needs of America's

TABLE 6.1 The top 20 American banks and the Cooke ratio: equivalent ratios in 1987

Banks	*1987 ratio*
J. P. Morgan	12·5
First Bank System	12·2
Fleet Norstar	12·2
Wells Fargo	10·9
FNC Financial	10·8
First Interstate	10·5
NBD	10·4
Suntrust Banks	9·7
Bank of Boston	9·6
Bankers Trust	9·4
NPNB	9·4
Security Pacific	9·3
Farnett Banks	8·9
Citicorp	9·3
First Chicago	7·9
Chase Manhattan	7·7
Mellon Bank	7·3
Bank of America	7·0
Manufacturers Hanover	6·9
Chemical	6·5

Source: Salomon Brothers, 1988.

top twenty banks vary between $5 bn, according to a study by Salomon Brothers in New York, and $10 bn according to another study by the International Banking and Commerce Association in London. The only point on which the two studies agree is that the banks with the most expansionist policies over the past twenty years are the ones that will have to make the most effort in the next few years. Among them are the Bank of America, which is still encountering serious problems, Manufacturers Hanover, First Chicago, Chase Manhattan, Continental Illinois, the Chemical Bank, and the Mellon Bank.

External difficulties

Following the problems of developing countries and the decline of real estate, commodity, and agricultural prices since 1980, a large number of banks have encountered difficulties. 1981 saw the beginning of what has become a growing trend in bank failures. Out of a total number of around 14,000 banks, 644 – 4.6 percent – went bankrupt between 1985 and 1988.

TABLE 6.2 American bank failures, 1981–1988

Year	*Number of failures*
1981	10
1984	79
1985	120
1986	160
1987	184
1988	180[a]

[a] Estimate.

The industrial crisis has also had an influence on the health of America's large banks. The case of Continental Illinois in 1984 is the most tangible demonstration of this. Intervention by the FDIC amounted to $4.5 bn and the final cost was $1.7 bn. The growing prevalence of mergers and takeovers is facilitated by the increasing obsolescence of what has been the administrative yoke on banking, the Glass–Steagall Act, which set up barriers between the large deposit banks and stock-market activities, as well as legislation that has compartmentalized banking and insurance activities. It seems that recent trends favor deregulation of the banking sector, a movement that will be especially welcomed by bankers, since it will enable them to do business on some very profitable market sectors. The movement has begun in the insurance sector: already twenty-eight American states have granted some or all banks partial or total access to the exercise of the insurance trade.

However, the American authorities will have to act in the area of regulation to comply with the principle laid down on 19 June 1989 by the European Economic Community on reciprocity in banking within the EEC. They have committed themselves strongly to obtain a non-restrictive text.

The American banking world has been badly shaken by the debt crisis of developing countries, to which it is greatly committed. Two figures are illustrative of the burden of this constraint.

In 1987, America's top 200 banks had some $30 bn in reserves for default on developing-country loans. The losses on Third World debt recorded by the six leading banks were only offset by the 1987 gains of the United States' seventy other largest banks. The ratio of exposure of American banks to developing-country risk, calculated according to the banks' capitalization, varies between 93 percent and 199 percent. For British banks, the margin is 27 percent–82 percent. Japan's banks are in a somewhat better position, with a ratio below 55 percent, except for the Bank of Tokyo. It is therefore easier to understand why the American authorities want to monitor closely the Third World debt problem and why an American bank (generally Citicorp) continues to play the leading role in defining a common approach to be adopted by major banks around the world. However, since early 1989, it seems that non-American authorities and commercial banks are questioning both the direction taken and the methods used, without being able to develop and implement a credible alternative.

TABLE 6.3 Developing-country exposure of commercial banks, 1988

Country	*Loans to developing countries/capitalization (%)*
United States	93–199%
United Kingdom	27–82%
Japan	under 55%

The ups and downs of new markets: The Drexel case

The rise, decline, and eventual collapse in February 1990 of the American firm Drexel Burnham Lambert is intimately linked to the evolution of the market in "junk bonds," securities for which both risk and yield are particularly high.

The origins of the junk bond market go back to 1981. Since then it has been playing a major role in the financing of highly leveraged acquisitions of both listed and unlisted companies. Typically, the buying company, which may be only a private partnership, takes over the target company through a financing structure the cost of which is charged to the latter. It would partly consist of junk bonds whose yield on issue would be 3.5 percent to 4.0 percent higher than that on Treasury bonds of the same maturity, and whose market yield has been as high as 22 percent in US dollars. Junk bond financings, therefore, help raiders to achieve their goals, but also imply that the target company can rely upon an operating cash flow which covers the financial cost of the takeover without detracting from the capacity of the firm to pursue its investment policy. These conditions have proved impossible to fulfil in many cases, even if further cash is derived from the liquidation or disposal of non-strategic assets and business lines. The financial charges incurred from the junk bonds sometimes represent up to 50 percent or even 100 percent of the free cash flow of the issuing company. This itself may be unbearable, but on top of that, the company's activity may decline or interest rates may go up. Then comes a liquidity crisis or even bankruptcy.

An economic microanalysis will locate the collapse of Drexel in the context of the financial structures adopted by the firm and its competitors.

Typically, Drexel would have built up the takeover financing as follows:

- 10 percent in equity,
- 20 percent in discount facilities,
- 40 percent in long-term banking debt,
- 30 percent in subordinated debt (junk bonds),

and would have signed a "highly confident letter," stating Drexel's confidence in its own ability to bring together all the necessary funds, which constitutes in itself a best effort commitment or even a commitment to succeed. This, in turn, would have given the raiders credibility.

In this way Drexel set up high-risk finance with insufficient attention to the underlying economic parameters of the acquisitions, with consequent adverse effect on both Drexel and the target companies when the market price of the bonds fell and when Drexel was simultaneously committed to propel the secondary market, which sometimes obliged them to repurchase the paper in a falling market.

Drexel's competitors felt the danger of such letters: in the transition period during which junk bonds were still issued in order to finance the acquisitions on a long-term basis, they preferred to grant bridging loans rather than committing themselves to raising long-term debt. Nevertheless, the financial charges incurred by such borrowings were so high that a number of bridging loans could not be repaid, thus creating an urgent need for refinancing through junk bonds, which were themselves less and less easy to place with investors.

In 1984, when the junk bond issues amounted to $15 bn in the United States, Drexel Burnham Lambert had 68 percent of the market. In 1986, these issues came to a peak of $41 bn and Drexel still accounted for 43 percent of them, although competition had intensified from other American investment banks, keen to play a role in the junk bond market because of its high profitability.

As early as 1987, difficulties arose in the repayment or refinancing of maturing junk bonds, and as a consequence of general discomfort on the part of both the financial institutions and the target companies, new issues slowed down from $36 bn in 1987 to $30 bn in 1988 and $28 bn in 1989.[1] At that time, Drexel Burnham Lambert's market share was 33 percent.

Drexel's decline began to accelerate in December 1988, when Drexel pleaded guilty to six felony counts relating to securities fraud and agreed to pay a record $650 m in fines and restitution. These violations of the Security and Exchange Commission's securities law jeopardized Drexel licenses in many American states; these could have been revoked because of the firm's record as an admitted felon. Simultaneously, and although stock option schemes or Drexel shares represented a large proportion of the remuneration of employees at all levels, Drexel experienced a heavy drain on its staff, who numbered 10,300 at the end of 1988, 9,220 in April 1989, and 5,500 in September the same year. These departures and redundancies in their turn considerably weakened Drexel's financial structure and decreased its net worth, for employees shares at the end of 1988 represented 58 percent of Drexel's market capitalization (US $1.9 bn).

Drexel had made profits of $522.5 m in 1986 on total revenues of $5.3 bn, but incurred a net loss of $166.7 m in 1988 after penalties of $650 m. The estimated loss for 1989 is $40 m on shrinking revenues of $4.1 bn.

On 13 February 1990, Drexel Burnham Lambert filed for bankruptcy protection after a group of banks refused to give it an emergency $350–400 m line of credit. This allowed the firm to seek temporary protection from its creditors so that it could continue to operate at least in some form.

On 23 April 1990, as the last episode of this progressive collapse, the head of Drexel's junk bonds department, who had been operating from California since 1978 and had resigned in June 1989, was personally fined $600 m. At the time of writing he faces the possibility of a jail sentence.

The Drexel episode epitomizes the dangers and shortcomings of a purely financially driven approach which privileges short-term gains benefiting mainly the management and the financiers, with little consideration for the long-term industrial dimension which requires stability and the allocation of available cash flow to finance new productive investment.

Shifts in market share

A study by the Federal Reserve Bank of New York[2] concerning market shares of multinational banks underlines a declining presence on the credit market, principally on the so-called wholesale market.

In 1974, some 30 percent of these banks were present on the credit market. In 1985, this proportion was no more than 25 percent. The reasons for this decline are numerous. Amounts outstanding in Treasury and municipal bonds have fallen, while the bank's share in the debt of households has remained constant, the decline in certain types of products being offset by an increase in other credits: mortgage credit, for example, grew from 30 percent in 1979 to 36 percent in 1984. On the other hand, consumer credit for durable goods witnessed a decline in the early 1980s, mainly on account of loans to industrial firms. The overdraft system of revolving credit has also steadily developed, fostered by the now widespread use of the credit card.

The percentage of banks present on financial services markets is difficult to evaluate. However, a few facts are worth mentioning. First, the takeover by a leading bank of one of the largest brokers in the United States has increased by 50 percent the bank's share in the brokerage earnings of brokers affiliated with the New York Stock Exchange. In contrast, subscriptions by the banks to pension fund certificates, now managed independently, have gone down. The banks are authorized to invest in traditional municipal bonds, in municipal bonds destined for education and housing, and in private investments. The banks have accounted for up to 42 percent of the issues.

The decline of wholesale banking is one of the most startling changes in the banking business. In 1974, 43 percent of US commercial banks were active in wholesale banking; in 1985, only 27 percent. This decline in bank participation was to the benefit of traders and brokers on the bond markets – and foreign banks, who have now captured over 30 percent of the market.

Commercial banks have declined in this segment because companies with abundant liquid funds available can obtain rates which are generally more advantageous than those granted by the banks by providing assistance to other lenders. Indeed, the emergence of a growing number of financial instruments and the sophistication of management methods in the large firms are increasing the possibilities of financial gains made in this way. However, Volkswagen's loss of over $250 m in March 1987 serves as a reminder that money market activities and trading within a multinational company is not risk-free. In order to be successful, it must take place in a culture different from that of the industrial activity; it requires both dexterity and careful planning in internal control and in the choice of markets, products, and counterparties.

During the decade from 1975 to 1986, a number of players in the United States saw their profitability fall considerably. For the most part there were four types:

1 Insurance companies. From 1973 to 1984, damages and losses grew at a much faster rate than premiums as a result of the emergence of new risks, with considerable damages awarded to a growing range of users or consumers, and a widespread tendency of policy beneficiaries to be less vigilant in reducing risks covered by insurance policies. From 1985 to 1990 the reverse trend seemed to apply.
2 Savings and loan associations. Several reasons account for their near-bankruptcy, including
   - loans granted at fixed rates and refinanced at variable rates;
   - lack of rigor in selecting customers;
   - decline of the real estate market with its associated effect on the value of securities;
   - excessively high management costs and poor management;
   - heavy involvement in LBOs.
3 Banks specializing in agriculture, real estate credit, and

credits to the energy industry. Losses in these sectors have been considerable, as we can see from the number of bank failures over the past seven years.

4 Multinational commercial banks, which saw their margins on commercial loans collapse while the need for reserves for doubtful debts of a commercial nature and on developing countries rose considerably.

At the root of these various declines are a number of common factors, including the inability to anticipate, indeed to perceive at all, profound and lasting market transformations and the difficulty in advancing from the diagnosis stage to the internal transformations needed in order to be able to create added value in this new environment. This requires re-examination of methods used in marketing, in evaluating risks and in monitoring costs per segment of activities.

On the other hand, some American banks have experienced remarkable development during this period. These include some regional banks, which have striven for ten years now to practice the trade of banker with all the severity that this implies,[3] a few merchant banks, in particular Morgan Stanley and Lazard New York, and certain insurance companies and financial conglomerates.

In general terms, the trend in financial profit in the United States shows that profitability rates are high for high-quality investment banks, regional banks, and for firms which finance consumer credit and mortgage credit, while results for other non-bank financial enterprises vary from one year to another and among the various institutions. However, for them, in real terms, the profitability trend is declining.

Cumulative commitment on high-risk transactions

The figures shown in table 6.4 underline the extent of the outstanding high-risk debt held by the American banks and illustrate their propensity to go for immediate financial gain rather than to invest patiently in expertise in ways that favor the growth of the US industrial fabric. They presage an even

TABLE 6.4 Financing by American banks of transactions involving a major leverage effect (at 30 June 1989)[a]

Bank	*Loans outstanding ($bn)*	*Commitments and/or investments ($bn)*	*Total ($bn)*	*Total, in % of equity, of loans using major leverage effect*	*Amounts outstanding on LDCs in % of equity*[b]
Citicorp	5·3	7·8	13·1	125	86
Chase Manhattan	3·0	4·3	7·3	144	106
J. P. Morgan	1·5	1·5	3·0	49	30
Bank of America	1·1	1·3	2·4	49	123
Chemical Bank	2·0	1·1	3·1	76	107
Manufacturers Hanover	3·7	1·7	5·4	162	192
Bankers Trust	3·2	3·7	6·9	193	81
Bank of New York	3·9	2·0	5·9	192	50
First Chicago	1·2	2·4	3·6	139	42
Continental	2·1	1·4	3·5	204	64

[a] High-risk transactions including a major leverage effect include leveraged buy-outs and the financing and refinancing by junk bonds of takeover bids.

[b] Net of provisions; in the case of Morgan, including the increase in provisions announced in September 1989.

Source: Keefe Bruyette & Woods.

greater decline of some of the larger American banks which will inevitably be forced to reduce their scope of intervention or to give up certain high-quality assets – as, for example, in the sale of 60 percent of Manufacturers Hanover's subsidiary, CIT, to Dai Ichi Kangyo Bank for $1,280 bn in September 1989. The current difficulties of First Bank System are symptomatic of this fragility of a part of the American banking system – ironically the part traditionally considered to be the most solid. This trend must be evaluated in the context of difficulties encountered by numerous merchant banks in the United States as well as the crisis of the savings and loan banks.

THE EUROPEAN BANKS

The 1989 agreement: A new structure

The contents

The EEC agreement concluded on 19 June 1989 lays down the structure which will regulate Europe's banks.

The principles decided are very liberal:

- the same authorization, or single approval, will be applicable for all banks, without exception, established in one of the member states before the deadline of 1 January 1993;
- these activities are not subject to surveillance solely by the supervisory authority of the country of origin.

The first thing to say is that this agreement definitely creates the status of European bank. This freedom of establishment granted to banks which obtain single approval will do away with national obstacles currently in effect and will simultaneously recharge competition among banks and open up new horizons to them. In the end these measures will probably increase the banks' potential customers five- or tenfold. So the stakes are considerable.

The second effect of the Directive involves reciprocity of rights granted to banks of non-member states. Some would have liked to benefit from the creation of the single market in order to obtain increased freedom of access to other financial markets. It seems that they did not succeed in winning their case, and the odds are that by the time the Directive goes into effect all the multinational banks will have adopted policies and taken measures to avoid being subject to the so-called reciprocity agreements.

As a side-effect the Directive will establish a hierarchy of European banks, consisting of three grades:

1 Those of a world status: the members of the future world banking oligopoly. Among these will be, for example, BNP, Deutsche Bank, and Barclays.
2 Those of a European status which will have a significant share of the market in Europe but will not have the necessary foundation to extend their activities to the rest of the world.
3 Those of a national and/or regional status which will cover a geographical area with a certain unity in terms of language or common interests. Their activities will be devoted to all segments which are not of a European dimension. Examples of this are the Bank of Bilbao in Spain and Bayerische Vereinsbank in West Germany.

The consequences

In the context of these emerging plans, interested parties have over the past few years been formulating strategies for the development of European bank enterprises, aimed at gaining access to countries where they have hitherto had no presence. These strategies are various. At one end of the range is the simple exchange of capital investments: for example, the Europartners movement recently added to its list a new agreement between the West German Commerzbank and the Spanish Banco Hispano Americano. Similar agreements involve the French Crédit Lyonnais and the Italian Banco di Credito di Roma. At the other extreme are takeovers: the Deutsche Bank, for example, has acquired the Banca d'Americana d'Italia and Morgan Grenfell in the UK.

In view of the specificity of each market, the banks will not adopt systematically a single approach for the single market. Three approaches can in fact be distinguished:

1 the approach, favored by major banks in the United Kingdom, West Germany, and France, of acquiring foreign banks
2 the approach of the so-called intermediate banks, which are concerned with specializing in sectors of activity on a European scale or in a specific region that overlaps several borders;
3 the approach of banks whose objective is to institute a European network at lower cost.

Banks in the United Kingdom, which are in a strong position because of their experience and a very large financial market, are facing Europe's reorganization secure in their superiority. They are content to acquire bank enterprises to gain access to new markets: for example, Midland has bought up the investment banks Trinkaus & Burkhardt in West Germany and Euromobiliare in Italy, and NatWest has been similarly active in France.

Cross-border association between medium-sized banks is one way for them to benefit from the opening of their national frontiers. This will certainly be a case simply of normalizing already active relations and streamlining customer procedures. This process will favor the setting up of structures whose scope of action will cover all or part of Europe.

The principle of exchanging equity participations between banking institutions makes it possible to create loose structures that may be capable over time of generating a European network at lower cost. Large banks like Crédit Lyonnais, BNP, the Deutsche Bank, or even the Commerzbank and the Bank of Scotland have decided to take this route as a response to the opening of frontiers that carefully leaves open different options for the future. Such an approach raises the issues of unity of purpose and of management and hence of the quality of services to customers and of profitability.

In Western Europe, the trend these past twenty years has

been of a steep net decline of the leading British banks mainly to the benefit of the West German and Japanese banks. It goes without saying that the banks have either greatly benefited or suffered from the fate of their country's economic power. The effects of the real economy on the financial and banking economy have been all the more evident because in Britain the banks operate in a climate of deregulation whereas in West Germany the banking market is closely protected from competition and there are considerable reciprocal shareholdings between banks and other enterprises. We find, therefore, within Europe the same phenomenon as has occurred between the United States and Japan, with the transfer of power between two countries' banks. From a theoretical point of view, it would be interesting to measure the strength and profitability of a country's banking sector on the basis of three criteria:

- the impact of individual bank strategies on the industrial fabric in the home country;
- the quantitative impact of surpluses or chronic deficits on the current balance of payments on the profitability of a domestic banking system;
- the approach to internationalization and its impact on bank profitability.

In addition to the transfer of banking power between two powers, which brings us back to the theory of speculation and in particular zero-sum speculation, there is a development which cannot pass unnoticed: namely, that France's banking sector is standing its ground in a very unstable environment while the country's economy seems to be evolving in the same way as the rest of the group of principal European economic powers. The fact that the banking sector is protected from competition, that it has developed in an oligopolistic national competitive universe, to a large extent explains this situation. However, we still need to ask whether the French banking structure is representative of the future of world banking, and whether the global oligopoly being formed will base itself on the competitive advantages of each national banking pole.

European banks have a heavy schedule ahead of them,

toward very precise deadlines with regard to the world hierarchy. Ridding themselves of rather inhibiting national restraints that are not, however, without their advantages, will expose them in most cases to stronger competition and a higher risk related to their activities. Measurement of efficiency using the ratio of profit to the number of employees will be an initial element of their response. European banks are particularly handicapped in this respect, although they are capable of achieving good results in terms of return on capital; they are far behind the Japanese banks and just short of the American banks, disregarding the poor results of the latter because of the very large reserves to cover developing-country commitments. Most European banks are overstaffed, principally, it seems, because of their extensive branch networks.

Deregulation is on the agenda in Europe and the first measures taken along these lines have left considerable dents in the operating accounts of companies. The "Big Bang" in London, for example, left Crédit Lyonnais with losses totalling Fr603 m in the accounts of its London subsidiary, Alexander Laing & Cruickshank. Nevertheless, there was some reorganization, which in the case of Crédit Lyonnais meant the sale of the exchange brokers CL–Astaire Co. Ltd, and the refocusing of its activities on its subsidiary Crédit Lyonnais Capital Markets Ltd. The results of the London merchant banks have been no better. Profit growth is low, with the remarkable exception of S. G. Warburg, Schroeders, and Hanson, while Morgan Grenfell and Kleinwort Benson's profits before taxes were down in 1987/8 for the second year in a row by 81.4 percent and 240 percent respectively. Taking all five of these merchant banks together, pre-tax profits fell by 17.7 percent between 1987 and 1988. These results are bringing about a constant reorganization of companies and rationalization of activities in order, on the one hand, to achieve better profitability, and on the other, to reduce overstaffing after the stock market crash of October 1987. In contrast, 1989 results have been outstanding, in particular, again, Warburg, Lazard, and Morgan Stanley, reflecting the quality of the culture and of the management team.

The Cooke ratio

Apart from profitability, commercial deposit banks must bring their operations into step with the Cooke ratio. Looking at banks in terms of geographical location, the European banks, at the end of 1987, had the least still to do in this respect. From the representative sample of Japan, the United States, and Europe, we obtain a higher arithmetic average for Europe while in the two other zones the ratio of equity to assets is falling. A few European banks have already gone over the 8 percent mark: BNP, for example, reached 8.3 percent at the end of 1988. The banks seem to be still waiting for the Bank for International Settlements to state its position before taking a stand on the issue of such securities as perpetual notes. BNP has renounced its $400 m (Fr2.72 bn); while Crédit Lyonnais is continuing its issue of $350 m (Fr2.4 bn). In the United Kingdom, Barclays Bank and Standard Chartered have made share issues of £903 m and £303 m respectively to restore their capital and bring themselves in line with the Cooke ratio.

British banks are in general fairly confident in their ability both to meet the stipulations of the Bank for International Settlements and seize the opportunities offered by the London financial market.

Opportunities in the London financial markets

Deregulation in the United Kingdom has brought regroupings, transfers, and takeovers on the London financial market.

The reorganization of the London financial markets

The British government's plans to modernize and reform the City's financial markets have led to a series of agreements with the Stock Exchange which have been gradually elaborated since 1983 and which resulted at the end of 1987 in a new organization of markets. The City's three traditional sectors – Stock Exchange markets, markets regulated by the Bank of

England, and international bonds markets – are now subject to new terms of operation.

This reform, by allowing the merger in 1983 between the Stock Exchange and the International Security Regulatory Organization (ISRO), has made the Stock Exchange the presiding organization not only for the British stock market but also for the international securities market. One should not lose sight of the fact that this measure is part of a wider outlook whose main aims are on the one hand to reinforce the role of international financial operators on the British market, and on the other to provide British institutions with the means to equip themselves with an international strategy by departitioning the market. The International Stock Exchange of the United Kingdom and the Republic of Ireland, an organization comprising 225 member firms of the Stock Exchange and 187 members of the ISRO, will see its governing body come increasingly under the control of large international firms. Proof of this exists already in the participation of fifty-six ISRO members in the Stock Exchange.

The Stock Exchange is organized in four sectors: domestic shares, international equities, options, and bonds. One of the new measures consists in doing away with the distinction between stockbrokers and counterparts. Now, the same players perform simultaneously the function of counterpart and intermediary; and the elimination of fixed broker fees reintroduces a negotiating dimension in the relationship with the customer.

The domestic shares market groups together the official quotation with the second and third market. At the end of 1985, the official quotation represented £245 bn. A new quotation assistance and information system was introduced at this time; hitherto, securities had been traded freely between counterparties and brokers, counterparty quotations simply being displayed as an indication. This system has now been complemented by the Stock Exchange Automated Quotation (SEAQ) which operates in the following manner:

- quotations are introduced into the SEAQ system by counterparties;

- business is concluded over the telephone between counterparties and customers;
- quotations are disseminated to members of the Stock Exchange and to outside subscribers.

There are plans for a second automatic quotation system to handle smaller orders. Market transformations will undoubtedly result in higher commissions having to be paid by small shareholders, while institutional investors will be able to negotiate particularly low rates.

The second market, worth £3.7 bn in market capitalization at the end of 1985, is also seeing the redistribution of roles between operators. The third market is open to securities not traded or traded very little on the over-the-counter market, provided that companies fulfil the necessary security conditions and go through an accredited intermediary.

The International Equities Market will be an important arena. The Stock Exchange has noted the development of trading on the over-the-counter markets in London between international operators using private network computer systems. It is to thwart these initiatives that the Stock Exchange has created SEAQ International as a forum for trade among the principal players in the international equities market, members of ISRO. This will institute the most liquid market on which the world's principal securities are traded.

The traded options market, on which approximately sixty counterparties trade some thirty instruments, that is, over 250,000 contracts per day, is undergoing rapid expansion.

The British bond market can be divided into three segments:

1. The government bond market (gilt market).
2. The domestic bond market, which groups together issues by local authorities, issues by companies, and issues in sterling by foreign organizations subject to the Stock Exchange's quotation system.
3. The Eurobond market, which, with approximately £200 bn in trading per year, is the favorite arena of international financial institutions whose decision-making centers are outside the United Kingdom, and whose activity is con-

> sequently not subject to control by the Stock Exchange but placed under the authority of an organization created for this purpose. Its task is to issue authorizations and to intervene in the framework of directives issued by the Association of Futures Brokers and Dealers which groups together at present 142 firms.

The transformation of the London financial market is not the result solely of financial market reform but also of changes on the money market, which was little affected by these reforms. The function of the central bank on the money market has remained virtually unchanged both on the interbank market – where the Bank of England does not intervene – and on the discount market, where it performs open market operations. The creation of new monetary instruments and the extension of the range of activities of discount houses, the intermediaries between the central bank and the commercial banks, constitute the new elements in the monetary regulation apparatus.

The eight discount houses, which buy bills of exchange from the banks to refinance the Bank of England by transfer of Treasury bills, were authorized by the central bank to diversify into bonds, insurance, and commodity futures markets. Four of them are at present controlled by international groups. The way is therefore now open to other institutions to enter what has up until now been a restricted area, intermediation between the interbank market and the Bank of England.

The government and domestic bond market, which accounts for 70 percent of the trading volume of London's financial markets, although it only constitutes 12 percent of capitalization, has also been undergoing modernization, with, on the one hand, the abolition of the two separate categories of stock market firms – the brokers and the "jobbers" (the latter being able to act as market-makers to the brokers who, in turn, intermediated with the investors) and, on the other, the granting of market-making licenses to twenty-seven firms (known as Gilt-edged Market Makers (GEMMs)). This ended the virtual market-making monopoly of Akroyd & Smithers and Wedd Durlacher.

Of the twenty-seven market-makers which replaced the jobbers, four are affiliates of deposit banks, four are brokerage houses and four are affiliates of merchant banks – not to mention the international arms of firms such as Crédit Suisse, First Boston, Merrill Lynch, Morgan Stanley, and Salomon Brothers.

The futures markets for financial instruments provide the counterparties with a means to cover their exposures to the Forex markets as well as the "cash" bound and money markets. Their reorganization, a decisive plank in the City's reform, will take as its model the existing London International Financial Futures Exchange (LIFFE) created in 1982. The contracts traded on LIFFE include Eurodollar and, recently, Eurodeutschmark, deposit contracts and German government bond contracts (*bund*).

Reinforcement of the current system's security implies widespread changes in the London Metal Exchange (LME). Negotiating methods have come under criticism because the price quoted only serves as an indication now that the contracting parties negotiate bilaterally and without a difference between cash and settlement prices. This is harmful to market transparency and flow. Furthermore, the bilateral nature of the exchanges and the absence of a clearing house pose security problems.

The recent reform of the London Commodity Exchange (LCE) has improved the structures, quotation mechanisms, and settlement system. Conditions are likely to be favorable to new entrants.

The remodelling of structures of these markets and the accompanying regulatory reform have led to regroupings, takeovers, and acquisition of holdings.

Regrouping movements

Regroupings were dictated by the need to bolster the financial and human means demanded by world competition. For the large banks it means above all taking advantage of opportunities offered by the British stock market, international investments, and the bond market. The British stock market appears to be an important arena now that interdependence, indeed, the interweaving of issuing and investment activities, has been recognized by international regulatory reform. This has resulted in three British clearing houses and a dozen merchant banks positioning themselves on this market segment.

Fund management constitutes a priority objective: the amount of funds managed in London now stands at over £250 bn, of which approximately 15 percent is of international origin. The Union des Banques Suisses has acquired Phillips & Drew which was managing nearly £6.5 bn at the end of September 1987.

British brokers' expertise in international investment varies. Certain institutions though, such as Quilter Goodison, Hoare Govett and James Capel, could play a very important role in the future; this probably explains why they were taken over by Paribas, Security Pacific (California) and Hongkong & Shanghai Banking Corporation (Hong Kong) respectively.

Acquisitions

British, American, and European banks have all been involved in takeovers. Only a few British groups have decided to favor endogenous growth: Lloyds Merchant Bank, Schroeder Wagg, Robert Fleming, Lazard Brothers, and Cazenove. The others made acquisitions. NatWest Investment Bank (NWIB) acquired, with an initial investment of £35 m, the broker Fielding Newson-Smith and the jobber Bisgood Bishop; it also made an initial investment of £44 m in British brokerage activities and over £25 m in state bonds. It operates in London, Tokyo, Hong Kong, Sydney, and New York. Barclays De Zoete Wedd (BZW) acquired the broker De Zoete & Bevan and the jobber Wedd Durlacher. Despite its traditional role as a commercial bank, it has been more successful than others in developing merchant bank activities, achieving a well-judged balance between the quality of teams, their decision-making autonomy, and the requirements of rigorous control. The merchant bank Samuel Montagu, a subsidiary of the Midland Bank, acquired

W. Greenwell and Smith Keen Cutter and no jobber. The initial investment amounted to some £30 m for market-making in UK equities and £25 m for the GEMM. Three years later, the total investment represented a multiple of these sums. In spring 1987 the Midland Bank decided to withdraw from the equities activity where it covered approximately 440 stocks in order to concentrate essentially on bond trading. Finally, Morgan Grenfell acquired Pember & Boyle (broker) and Pinchin Denny (counterpart) at the price of £30 m. Morgan Grenfell, less international than the other merchant banks, only intervenes on the financial markets of London and Europe.

At the time of writing eleven foreign groups have been involved in acquisitions: Citicorp, American Express (Shearson Lehman), Chase Manhattan, Union des Banques Suisses, Royal Bank of Canada, Nomura, Crédit Suisse, Hongkong & Shanghai Banking Corporation, Merrill Lynch, Security Pacific, and Paribas. Citicorp acquired Vickers Da Costa and Scrimgeour Kemp-Gee at a cost of £75 m, thus reinforcing its presence on financial markets throughout the world: London, Europe, New York, Latin America, Hong Kong, Singapore, Tokyo, Asia, Sydney, and Melbourne. American Express bought the broker L. Messel for £20 m. However, it has favored a targeted approach to its market activities and has concentrated on three markets: London, New York, and Tokyo. Chase Manhattan acquired Simon & Coates and Laurie Milbank and traders on the world's major markets. Union des Banques Suisses, Royal Bank of Canada, Crédit Suisse, Hongkong & Shanghai, Merrill Lynch, Security Pacific, and Paribas each acquired a single broker. They acquired in this way Phillips & Drew, Kitcat & Aitken, Buckmaster & Moore, James Capel, Giles & Cresswell, Hoare Govett, and Quilter Goodison respectively. Goldman Sachs operates on the world's main financial markets in direct competition with Citicorp and the Chase Manhattan Bank through its operations in London, Europe, New York, Canada, Hong Kong, Singapore, Melbourne, and Sydney as well as in other countries in Asia. Paribas, by contrast, is rather judiciously positioned on two markets: London and continental Europe, and to a lesser extent, the United States and Japan. Salomon

Brothers and Goldman Sachs have not considered it necessary to make acquisitions in Europe and Japan.

As a result of acquisitions and integrations, all the leading stockbrokers, with the exception of Cazenove, have been bought out: sixty-four of the City's 208 counterparts. Furthermore, nineteen of the top twenty changed hands, of which over ten are now owned by banks of world status. The terms of integration can be total or partial. There are three types:

1 Acquisition not followed by integration. The firm acquired retains its entire autonomy of management and makes only a simple reorientation of its activities. Such was the solution chosen by Security Pacific in the takeover of Hoare Govett.
2 The management of the acquired firm is integrated within the framework of a group policy. The legal forms of each establishment are maintained to preserve different styles of management and remuneration. This was the formula chosen by Paribas when it acquired Quilter Goodison, by Hongkong & Shanghai for James Capel and by UBS for Phillips & Drew.
3 The acquired entity is completely absorbed into the structures of the host group, with the employees being integrated into the branches and specialized departments of the parent company. Thus, National Westminster has regrouped under a single management the County Bank, the counterpart Bisgood Bishop, and the stockbroker, Fielding Newson Smith. We should also mention Warburg Securities, which now co-ordinates the group's securities activities after acquiring the two brokers Rowe & Pittman and Mullens and the jobber Akroyd & Smithers. They also regrouped all the fund management activities under the authority of one company, Mercury Asset Management.

Acquisition and more or less complete integration is the policy of Britain's leading commercial banks: Barclays, NatWest, and Midland. The Royal Bank of Scotland has also chosen the same path; Lloyds, however, continues to go it alone and has bought no stockbroker or counterpart.

Likewise, it is worth noting that while seven merchant banks

(Kleinwort Benson, Warburg, Hill Samuel, Morgan Grenfell, Brown Shipley, Guinness Peat, and Baring Brothers) have taken over brokers and jobbers, two of them (Schroeders and Robert Fleming) have favored a policy of endogenous development of these activities, while yet others – Lazard, Hambros, Société Générale – have either limited their investment (Hambros and the Société Générale in the case of the broker Strauss Turnbull) or stayed out. It is worth noting the reticent attitude of the insurance companies toward amalgamation, with the exception of Commercial Union, whose position is in contrast to the policy adopted by the financial (Mercantile House), industrial (British & Commonwealth), and commercial (Sale Tilney) groups.

The degree of involvement of the world's large groups should be underscored: fewer than twenty financial groups accounting for 30 percent of world issues have opted for a policy of acquisition. Several reasons can be found for this.

The North American firms have adopted a very reserved attitude: only three US and one Canadian firm have made direct investments. Citicorp acquired the broker Scrimgeour Vickers; Chase, Laurie Milbank and Simon & Coates; Security Pacific, Hoare Govett; the Royal Bank of Canada, Kitcat & Aitken.

It is noteworthy that the Japanese banks have not engaged in any takeover moves (although Nomura did apply for membership in the Stock Exchange) and that an agreement between the ISRO and the London Stock Exchange has enabled forty-four Japanese banks and securities firms, members of the ISRO, to become members of the new institution.

The French, Swiss, and German banks have been notably active. Paribas bought Quilter Goodison; Crédit Commercial de France, Laurence Prust; the Union des Banques Suisses bought the broker Phillips & Drew; Crédit Suisse bought Buckmaster & Moore and Harold Rattle. On a smaller scale, the Société Générale has maintained a 30 percent investment in Strauss Turnbull, whereas BNP has limited itself to promoting the creation of its own brokerage firm. The Deutsche Bank, which up to 1990 had only a 5 percent interest in Morgan Grenfell, took control of the entire group in that year.

This analysis of the reorganization of the London financial market would not be complete without underlining the difficulties involved in rapidly and fully absorbing teams of brokers into larger groups. Differences in company culture lead to problems of motivation, communication, and customer relations. Cases of failure are not rare, as demonstrated by massive defections of entire teams. Success requires a highly differentiated style of personnel management and a long-term effort to adjust established mind-sets.

THE JAPANESE BANKS

The particular characteristics of the Japanese banks and of their international activities owe much to the role played by the public authorities – but also to wise strategic decisions and favorable external factors.

The public authorities and Japanese banks

It can never be stressed enough that Japan's distinctive foreign economic policy was the subject of widespread national consensus among organizations of divergent interests but united by the same values and the same ends. This common will permeates the conduct of the Japanese elite as a whole: the Liberal Democratic Party, the Ministry of International Trade and Industry (MITI), and the Ministry of Finance (MOF), businessmen, and bankers.

The high degree of supervision of Japanese banks is another distinct characteristic linked to the determining role played by the MOF and the Bank of Japan: their control extends over areas as diverse as the creation of branches, opening hours, credit volume, interest rates, and accounting rules. The number and precision of these controls does not prevent the Japanese banks from being competitive. The close relationship between the banking circle and senior government officials who thrive on the same values makes it possible to elaborate policies that are in line with Japan's true long-term interest.

The recent example of Sumitomo Bank's acquisition of the Heiwa Sogo Bank, which Citicorp had its eye on, is full of lessons on the relations of collusion and goodneighborliness that exist between the banks and the Japanese authorities. These relations include a mode of conducting the elaboration and implementation of the country's foreign economic policy whereby the banks participate both as fully fledged members of the Japanese elite and as financial institutions of world status. This important economic role of the banks is demonstrated by the place they occupy in financing and organizing international trade, investing in international projects, and providing funds for the multinational firms.

The authorities of the Bank of Japan and the International Finance Bureau maintain regular contacts with Japanese banks involved in international activities; these banks in turn maintain close relations with Japan's principal partners. Also, the government has recognized the banks' commercial legitimacy and implemented a range of incentives to develop their international activities. Among these is insurance, intended to encourage exports and investment abroad. In the early 1980s, interventions covered 40 percent of Japanese exports, which by international standards is a considerable proportion.

In addition, the Import–Export Bank of Japan, a government institution, not only participates in the joint financing, with the private banks, of numerous investments but also influences credit decisions. Its involvement in a project indicates the government's implicit approval of the investment. Approval by the Overseas Economic Co-operation Fund of an international investment means that it falls into the category of national investment and is automatically ensured a high level of security.

In return, the Japanese authorities have largely used the international activities of the country's banks and other financial institutions to exercise control over rates in a way that favors Japanese industry. For close on twenty years now, long-term capital flows have offset balance-of-trade movements.[4] Before the crisis of 1973, the government lifted restrictions on foreign investment financing by Japanese banks, thus, by allowing them access to the large currency reserves held by the Bank of

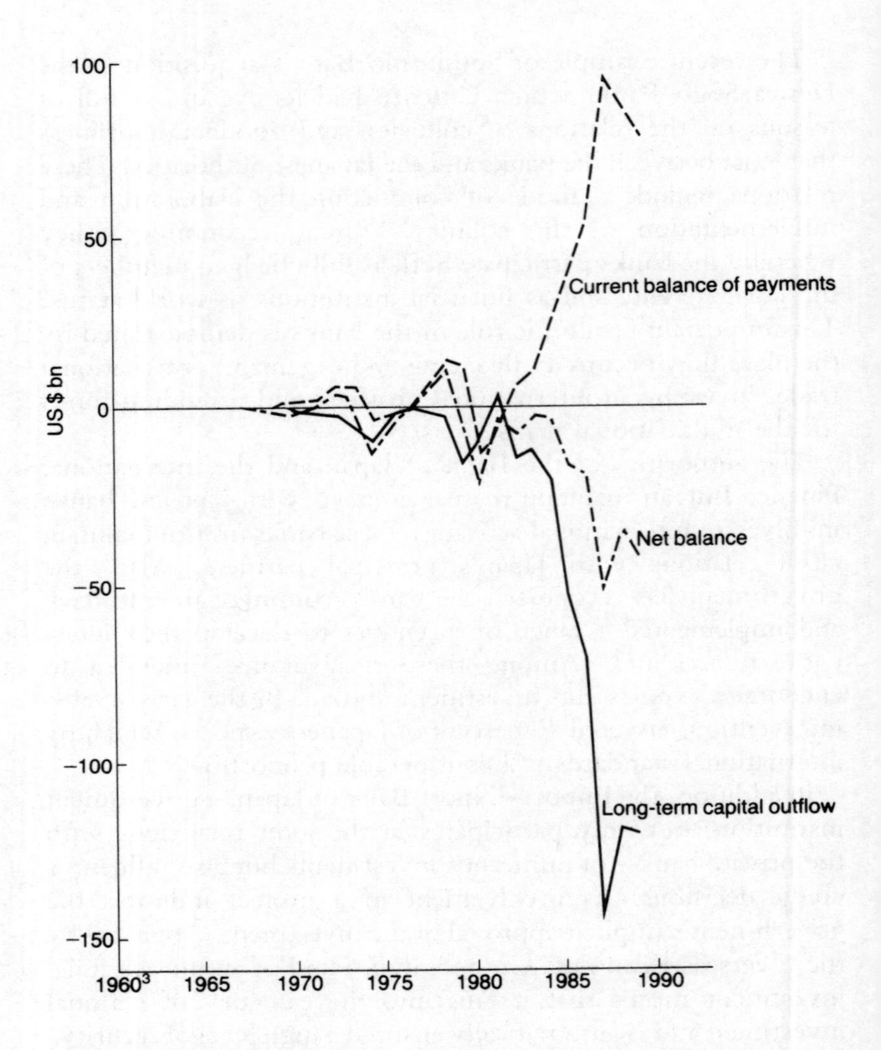

FIGURE 6.1 Movement of capital in Japan: current balance of payments minus long-term capital outflows
Source: Bank of Japan.

Japan, reducing their financing needs on the interbank foreign currency market. During the years of crisis from 1973 to 1975 measures were taken to limit capital flight. But from 1976, when the balance of accounts was showing signs of recovery, these measures were lifted and the Japanese banks became dynamic operators on the Euromarket.

Judicious strategic choices

The internationalization of Japanese banks is particularly striking because of its suddenness and irrepressible growth. What sets it apart are the decisions made both within the country, in reinforcing close relations with the entire Japanese industrial sector, which gets from the banks the support it needs, and abroad, in specializing in fast-growing sectors.

Since 1980, the Japanese banks' strategy has been founded on the volume effect: not systematically, in a common bid all to become universal world banks, but instead selecting a certain number of products or segments from the world financial market. This so-called strategy of "a thousand little steps" consists in concentrating on market slots that are sensitive to volume power and fragile in terms of price.

The Japanese banks first offered loans to governments and

TABLE 6.5 Japanese trade balance and movement of capital, 1974–1988

	Current balance ($bn)	*Dollar/yen exchange rate*	*Inflation rate (%)*	*Capital account (long-term)*
1974	−4·69	292·08	24·4	−3·88
1975	−0·68	296·79	11·8	−0·27
1976	3·68	296·55	9·3	−0·98
1977	10·92	268·51	8·0	−3·18
1978	16·53	210·44	3·8	−12·39
1979	8·75	219·14	3·6	−12·98
1980	−10·75	226·75	8·0	2·39
1981	4·77	220·53	4·9	−6·45
1982	6·85	249·08	2·7	−16·25
1983	20·80	237·51	1·8	−18·73
1984	35·00	237·52	2·3	−50·01
1985	49·37	238·54	2·0	−63·26
1986	85·83	168·52	0·6	−132·08
1987	87·00	144·64	0·1	−133·98
1988	79·59	128·15	0·7	−117·00

Source: International Finance Corporation – IMF.

corporates at interest rates hitherto unknown. Likewise, they shook the Eurobond market, but not without preventing Nomura from reaching second place on this market. More recently, they have penetrated merger and acquisition activities; their development here has been rapid, though less spectacular than in the first two slots. Today, they are more and more keen to expand world markets for all the financial products which are most directly linked to the healthy prosperity of Japan's economy: Euroyen bonds, warrant bond issues, etc.

The volume with which they are able to intervene is used to increase their market share – after, of course, destabilization has been brought about by waging a price war.

The amendment of banking legislation in Japan in 1980 set off the process of internationalization of the country's banks. Indeed, in the absence of domestic competition, financial deregulation came to be the outlet for competition before turning into the counterweight against it.

There are numerous reasons for this international expansion. Among them are:

- the internationalization of the yen, stimulated by deregulation of Japan's financial markets;
- the reduction of margins on the domestic market;
- the concern for loan diversification: for the past fifteen to twenty years, a large percentage of bank amounts outstanding has financed the purchase of securities and real estate.

In a strong position as a result of their industrial policy, the Japanese public authorities have indirectly procured a base for their banking and financial institutions which is the envy of many a European or American company of the same sector. In addition, the existence of very close ties between Japan's industrial firms and banks in the form of reciprocal shareholdings affords the banks access to a privileged clientele which they accompany in their developments abroad.

For cultural and political reasons Japan has one of the highest savings rates among Western countries (see table 6.6). This means that the banks have large amounts of liquidity to manage

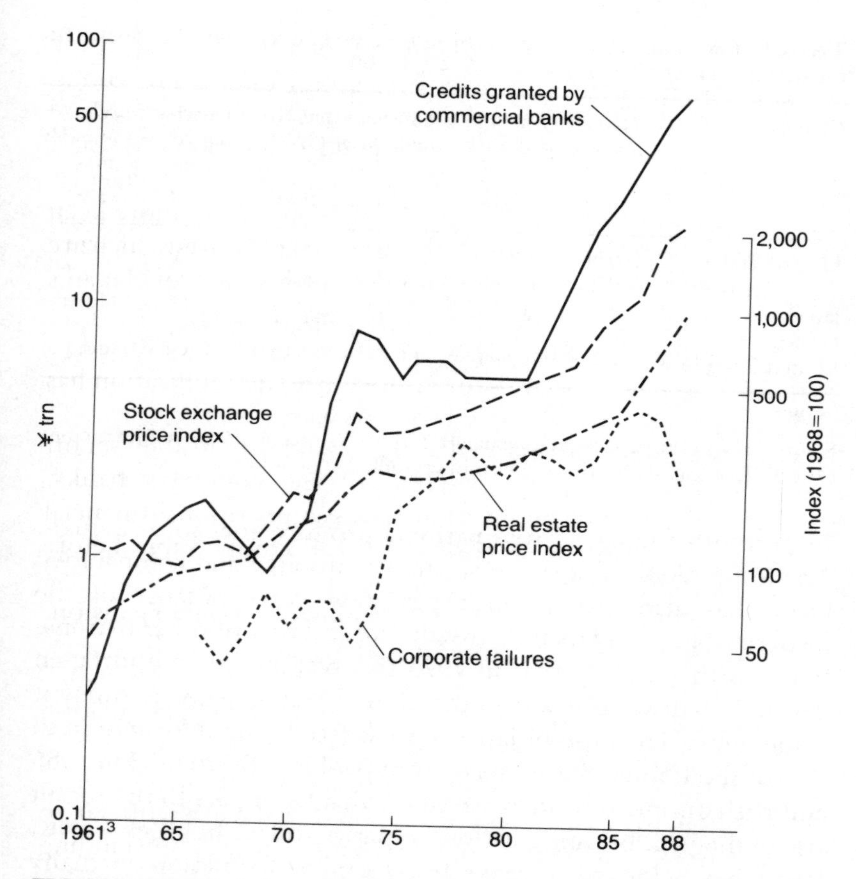

FIGURE 6.2 Evolution of the basic Japanese stock and real estate prices in relation to bank loans
Source: Bank of Japan, Tokyo Stock Exchange, Japan Real Estate Institute, Teikolu Data and Mikuni & Co., September 1989.

and thus a decisive competitive advantage in their international activities.

The savings rate for Japanese households has come down somewhat since 1973, but it still remains the highest in the world today at 11.4 percent. In relative terms, the gap with the United States has considerably widened: in 1974, the savings rate of Japanese households was nearly three times greater than the American; by 1987 it was nearly six times that amount; over

TABLE 6.6 Household and company savings rates and the financing capacity of public administration, 1974 and 1988

Country	*Household saving rate (% of GNP)*		*Company savings rate (% of GNP)*		*Financing capacity (+) or need (−) of public administration*	
	1974	*1988*	*1974*	*1988*	*1974*	*1988*
United States	6·56	2·96	1·36	1·65	−0·3	−2·1
West Germany	9·23	7.85	4·75	4·36	−1·3	−2·1
Japan	16·18	10·15[a]	0·62	2·18[a]	+0·4	+0·6[a]
France	14·10	8·47	8·62	10·07	+0·1	−1·1
United Kingdom	8·14	2·89	14·13	13·82	−3·8	+0·8

[a] 1987.

Sources: for savings, *Comptes nationaux trimestriels*, no. 4, 1989; for financing, *OECD Economic Perspectives*, December 1989.

18 percent of Japan's gross national product goes into savings. The importance of Japanese savings in absolute and comparative terms has also grown these past few years because of the disparity between Japan's growth rate and that of other nations. It is worth recalling that in 1973 the average income in Japan was only half what it was in the United States, whereas today it is the same. The ratio of Japan's gross fixed capital formation to that of the United States grew from 0.74 in 1974 to 0.83 in 1986 and has continued to increase since, thanks in part to the recent rise in the yen, bringing it close to parity today. In other words, Japan has achieved a gross fixed capital formation virtually equal to that of the United States with a population less than half the size.

The banks owe their strong expansion first and foremost to the exceptional capacity of the Japanese to save, a strength

TABLE 6.7 Ratio of savings to GNP, Japan and United States, 1980–1988 (%)

	1980	*1981*	*1982*	*1983*	*1984*	*1985*	*1986*	*1987*	*1988*
Japan	21·0	20·8	19·9	18·8	19·9	20·8	21·5	21·5	22·5
United States	7·0	7·5	3·0	2·5	5·0	3·8	2·8	2·5	3·5

Source: BIS.

which almost forces them to expand. Until the 1970s, Japanese savings found their natural outlet on the domestic market. Then, at the beginning of that decade, it was poured into the large public budget. Once these two receptacles had been filled, at the end of the 1970s, a savings surplus appeared on domestic investment (positive savings gap) which is now close to 3.5 percent of Japan's national product. Since then, it has remained at the absolute level of some $80 bn – 0.5 percent of world GNP.

It is noteworthy that this surplus is quite comparable, in absolute value, to that accumulated by the oil-producing countries in 1974 (approximately $100 bn) and that from a relative point of view (as a proportion of gross world product) it is equal to half that surplus. Such a savings overspill obviously means a risk of world economic deflation, as occurred in 1974 and 1979, unless immediate action is taken not only to invest but also to reinvest these amounts. It is precisely here that the Japanese banks have played a remarkable role, perhaps forced upon them to the extent that the domestic savings surplus is equal to the foreign trade surplus. This led the banks to play a role of intermediation. This becomes apparent if one compares the resources of commercial banks and their consequent uses in the United States and in Japan since 1973 (see tables 6.8 and 6.9).

The Japanese banks did not begin to develop their activities in any spectacular manner until 1980, when they took the place of the American banks, chronically handicapped by their excessive involvement in developing-country debt and later, in particular since 1985, in the financing of highly leveraged transactions. They did not limit themselves to "investing" their surplus domestic savings on the world market but adopted a policy of world intermediation, pitting themselves specifically in policy terms against the role held by the American banks in the 1970s.

The Japanese banks' accession to the highest ranks of the bank assets classification was therefore nothing more than proper recognition of Japan's emergence as the pre-eminent industrial power. Recent statements by the Japanese authorities in favor of Japan asserting its role in development aid schemes

TABLE 6.8 Uses and resources of US commercial banks

	Value ($bn)					Average growth rate (%)							
	1973	1979	1982	1985	1988	1973–9		1979–82		1982–5		1982–8	
						Nominal	Real	Nominal	Real	Nominal	Real	Nominal	Real
Call deposits	209	283	327	408	494	5·2	−3·1	4·9	−4·6	7·7	3·8	7·1	3·6
Fixed deposits	242	433	586	901	1,081	10.2	1·6	10·6	0·6	15·4	11·3	10·7	7·1
Overseas commitments	41	157	164	180	283	25·1	15·3	1·5	−7·7	3·2	−0·5	9·5	5·9
Others	221	430	671	717	924	11·7	3·0	16·0	5·5	2·2	−1·4	5·5	2·0
State and community debts	154	229	295	429	345	6·8	−1·5	8·8	1·0	13·3	9·3	2·6	−0·8
Private sector debts	496	887	1,146	1,539	2,137	10·2	1·5	8·9	−0·9	10·3	6·4	10·9	7·3
Overseas assets	27	140	264	190	235	31·6	21·3	23·6	12·4	−10·4	−10·0	−1·9	−1·9
Others and adjustment	36	47	43	48	65	4·5	−3·7	−2·9	−2·7	2·2	−1·4	7·1	3·6
Total resources/uses	713	1,303	1,748	2,206	2,782	10·6	1·9	10·3	0·3	8·1	4·2	8·1	4·5
Consumer price index	53·9	88·1	117·1	130·5	143·5	8·5		10·0		3·7		3·5	
GDP (constant prices)	2,344	2,734	2,714	3,073	3,418	2·6		−0·2		4·2		3·9	
Exports (current prices)	90	223	270	281	431	16·3		6·6		1·3		8·1	

Source: IFS–IMF.

Table 6.9 Uses and resources of Japanese commercial banks

	Value (¥bn)					Average growth rate (%)							
	1973	*1979*	*1982*	*1985*	*1988*	*1973–9*		*1979–82*		*1982–5*		*1982–8*	
						Nominal	*Real*	*Nominal*	*Real*	*Nominal*	*Real*	*Nominal*	*Real*
Call deposits	31,198	53,968	61,124	65,573	80,323	9·6	−0·4	4·2	−0·9	2·4	0·3	4·7	3·4
Fixed deposits	57,877	122,700	165,684	217,824	297,532	13·3	3·0	10·5	5·1	9·6	7·3	10·3	8·9
Overseas commitments	4,148	10,343	23,324	40,890	97,176	16·4	5·9	31·1	24·7	20·6	18·2	26·9	25·3
Others	23,381	47,022	53,571	75,967	89,738	12·3	2·1	4·4	−0·7	12·4	10·1	9·0	7·6
State and community debts	7,099	35,846	42,488	50,126	62,916	30·9	19·0	5·4	0·6	5·7	3·5	6·8	5·4
Private sector debts	103,246	187,492	241,718	318,501	430,125	10·5	0·4	8·8	3·5	9·6	7·4	10·1	8·7
Overseas assets	3,080	6,169	14,240	25,329	63,787	12·3	2·1	32·2	25·6	21·2	18·7	28·4	26·8
Others and adjustment	3,179	4,526	5,257	6,298	7,941	6·1	−3·6	5·1	−0·1	6·2	4·1	7·1	5·8
Total resources/uses	111,604	234,033	303,703	400,254	564,769	12·3	2·1	9·1	3·7	9·6	7·4	10·9	9·5
						1979/1973		1982/1979		1985/1982		1988/1982	
Consumer price index	52·4	92·6	107·8	114·6	116·2	10·0		5·2		2·1		1·3	
GDP (constant prices)	181,395	230,074	256,395	291,207	330,012	3·7		3·7		4·3		4·3	
Exports (current prices)	12,133	27,904	44,479	52,067	47,577	14·9		16·8		5·4		1·1	

Source: IFS–IMF.

reflect the country's financial strength and the maturity of its economic and financial system. We must also expect Japan to have a growing say in the decisions of the international organizations, in particular with regard to quotas set by the IMF and the World Bank. The power of the Japanese bank is almost certainly firmly established.

This whole evolution is no chance outcome: on the contrary, it is based on a cultural dimension whose roots run deep into Japan's past, in particular its history over the last 500 years. One of the intriguing problems facing this country now, and indeed any civilization at a comparable stage, is how it will spend the surplus wealth which it is accumulating at an unprecedented rate – a rate that is very likely to increase much more rapidly in the future than it has in the past.[5] The evolution of the results of the Dai Ichi Kangyo Bank is significant in this respect (see figure 6.3).

It is highly unlikely that the next twenty-five years will see any fundamental change in the Japanese way of life, which is based on hard work, unity of race and values cemented by 2,000 years of history, and a national will to rise to a level of world pre-eminence comparable to that of the United States in 1945. Under these conditions, it appears probable that Japan will

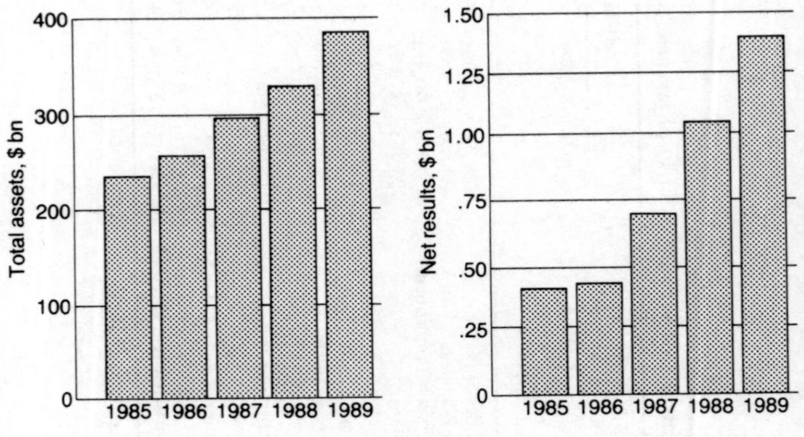

FIGURE 6.3 The Dai Ichi Kangyo Bank: assets and profitability, 1985–1989

continuè to direct a large share of its surplus wealth outside the country, mainly in the form of industrial and financial investments.

This approach has numerous advantages. Economic growth beyond Japan's frontiers is, reversing the Clausewitz formula, "the continuation of war by other means." A position of dominant financial power outside the country puts the Japanese in infinitely greater control of the pace of internal transformation of their society than if this wealth were for the most part invested at home. Control over the evolution of their culture through internal maturing, has always been one of the principal features of Japanese history. All the indications (their economic success, for one) are that the Japanese will continue the behavior that has enabled them to protect a national and cultural identity which is unquestionably one of the principal factors in their success.

However, the world dominance of Japanese banking cannot continue without provoking some resistance, especially from European countries. The Europe of the 1992 Single European Act is likely to deploy a co-ordinated strategy and policy to oppose any foreign penetration, and in particular that of banks.

Indeed, the EC will have to adopt a new position on foreign trade, with an increased role for the European Commission in defining such a policy. In the monetary and financial area, it seems inevitable that serious resistance will emerge to any significant or large-scale foreign penetration. Europe is entering a long period in which national policies must be realigned to create a co-ordinated financial and monetary policy which means, in the longer term, the use of a common currency and the creation of a central bank of central banks. It is understandable that under such circumstances the political authorities are extremely alert to the prospect of any significant foreign intrusion.

Moreover, it appears inevitable that the American banking sector's spectacular world decline will be the prelude to a phase of national concentration, followed ten to twenty years later by the emergence of an American oligopoly. From a base of this kind, it would be possible for American banks to attempt to jump back into the battle for the world market with more chance of competing efficiently, provided that they acknowledge the reasons for their past decline and develop solutions consistent with their culture and mentality.

Notwithstanding this, the Japanese banks are benefiting and will continue to benefit for a long time from a very favorable position which they are striving to maintain through adaptation.

Favorable external factors

The ineluctable growth of the purchasing power of the yen, which more than doubled in the 1980s, has been accompanied by a reinforcement of its place in the Japanese banks' foreign currency positions. In 1982, the dollar accounted for approximately 80 percent of these positions and the yen only 3 percent. In 1988, the dollar's share fell to 63 percent and the yen's rose to

TABLE 6.10 Exchange rates between the US dollar and other major currencies, 1982–1988

	1982	*1983*	*1984*	*1985*	*1986*	*1987*	*1988*	*% change 1982–8*
Dollar/yen	235	232	251	220	194	175	170	−34·6
Dollar/deutschmark	2·37	2·72	3·15	2·46	1·94	1·53	1·73	−24·9
Dollar/franc	6·72	8·34	9·59	7·56	6·45	5·34	6·05	− 8·8
Dollar/sterling	0·62	0·69	0·86	0·69	0·68	0·53	0·55	−10.9

Source: IMF.

TABLE 6.11 Distribution by currency of banks' foreign positions, 1982–1987[a]

Currency	*1982*	*1985*	*1986*	*1987*
Dollar	831	1,238·9	1,488·9	1,606·4
Yen	30	232	325·2	436·4
Deutschmark	160	124·2	223·7	445·6
Sterling	15·5	60·1	82·4	120·5

[a] Includes only those banks required to publish figures.
Source: BIS.

17 percent, the fall in one almost totally offset by the rise in the other: of the 17 percentage points lost by the dollar, the yen took 14. There are no signs at present to indicate that this trend is slackening – still less that a change in direction is imminent. Japan's surplus savings and its foreign trade surplus do not appear to have been at all diminished by the yen's successive revaluations. Japan seems, in fact, to have entered a virtuous circle of exchange. Furthermore, the United States has still not managed to balance its foreign trade and is experiencing a savings deficit.

It is to be expected that a growing number of both financial institutions (including banks of world status) and individuals, motivated by the desire for a safe investment or capital gain, will want to buy an increasing amount of financial assets in yen. This will in the years to come give the Japanese banks an extremely powerful incentive to extend their network of customers, as indeed they are already doing today on the west coast of the United States.

Furthermore, the Japanese banks seem the best placed to fulfil the criteria laid down by the BIS with regard to quality evaluation based on equity ratios and activity profitability. For Japanese bankers, 1988 will remain the year when they brought their ratio in step with international requirements. Taking advantage of the vitality of Japan's financial markets in 1988 to issue shares and/or convertible bonds for the amount of ¥2 trn (approximately £8.9 bn), the thirteen leading banks now have a ratio exceeding the 8 percent required for 1992.

The second BIS requirement, however, concerns the profitability of the banks' activity, and the profitability of the top five Japanese banks was only 0.22 percent in 1988 (against 0.48 percent for BNP). In order to satisfy this criterion, banks are going to have to increase their most profitable activities, that is, individual and small-company loans. The scheme most commonly chosen since 1960 is definitely out: loans to low profit-making large firms must no longer be allowed to erode bank profitability. Since the actual measurement is a ratio of profits to assets, the Japanese banks can also work toward the desired result by limiting asset growth. In 1988 they embarked on this path too, and their average annual asset growth rate has returned to 12 percent after an average rate of 18 percent between 1983 and 1987.

The BIS requirements encouraged the Japanese banks in 1983 to rethink their strategy with regard to accounting results, while legislative developments seemed to indicate that deregulation of the banking sector was imminent. Pressure for a new Article 65 of the Securities and Exchange Act became increasingly strong. At the beginning of 1989, the situation was already considerably advanced; bankers were authorized to create subsidiaries abroad to act as brokers while securities houses were granted the right to set up subsidiaries abroad to act as bankers. A legislative bill was presented to the Financial System Research Council (FSRC) which would involve authorizing the banks to trade in securities within the framework of bloc trading. (The retail trading of securities would remain forbidden.) If this bill is adopted, the banks will be able to exercise this activity in Japan within two to three years.

There is opposition between the four large securities houses on the one hand, criticized by institutional investors for taking 40 percent of the business, and the banks on the other. The balance so far seems to favor the latter, although compensation is being granted to the former. Securities house profits are behind the pressure to abandon legislation based on the American model, the Glass–Steagall Act. With the Industrial Bank of Japan already making 36 percent of its profit through its single brokerage activity on the trading of securities, it is possible that the complexion of the Japanese financial scene under deregulation may alter to the benefit of the banks and therefore to the detriment of the securities houses, despite their power.

7

◇

The Strategies

◆

THE BACKGROUND TO STRATEGY CHOICE

In the course of the past four decades, the weight of money in business has soared, as a result both of the increasing volumes dealt in and of the large number of new products and wide fluctuations. The internationalization and growth of financial activities which have resulted from the development of information technology in international trade and from the implosion of national regulations, now make this sector of economic activity a priority area for strategists.

Look at Napoleon's meditations on strategy: "Nothing is obtained in war but by calculation. In a campaign, anything that is not thought through in detail does not give results. Every expedition demands to be carried out according to a system." And: "Give a two-thirds chance to calculation and leave a third to fate." Two centuries later, Van Cauwenberg and Coch gave a more modern definition of strategy as "calculated conduct in an unprogrammed situation." In other words, strategy must fulfil certain conditions. It is up to those in charge to indicate clearly the strategic intent pursued, to estimate the means and resources of competitors, to acquire thorough knowledge of people and circumstances, to foresee successes in order to take advantage of them, to plan for setbacks in order to overcome them. Finally, *they must ensure that fundamental analyses are factually accurate.*

In our day and age, however, this methodology, which dates

back a few centuries, is no longer enough. Strategy no longer depends solely on the knowledge of a few strategists, but on the behavior of every person within the organization. Strategic behavior at every level of the bank, from the chief executive officer down to the most junior employee, is now becoming the key factor of success. If this approach is to be adopted, there must be more basic work of a greater depth within banks, because goals and objectives can be many and contradictory, ranging from the simple search for profit to the capture of new market share.

A bank's strategy should be defined as "a strategic intent broken down into a set of values, objectives, and policies requiring a relentless concern with implementation." If banking, like war, is all the "art of execution," in an environment undergoing wide-ranging, abrupt transformations, strategy defines the ideal road it must follow in order to specify and control its relation with its environment.

Strategy of conquest, strategy of change, strategy of consolidation – these are the three roads taken by the principal players in the national and international banking sector. However, there is rarely one uniform approach throughout a firm. Certain poles of activity will be based on an offensive strategy, whereas others will consolidate the experience of or even abandon market segments or products considered to have no future. Banking reality is the coexistence of a multitude of strategies – essential where markets are so diverse and fluctuating – and in the pre-eminence of a main theme which sets the dominant tone.

The diversity of strategies currently being deployed can be seen from a look at the desire for world conquest of such banks as Citicorp, the Deutsche Bank, Barclays, and the ten leading Japanese banks; the consolidation strategies of the Morgan Guaranty Trust, of NatWest, and of the large French commercial banks; and the strategies of change of the Commerzbank and of Continental Illinois. Whatever the case, every strategy must be based on a vision. The absence of vision constitutes the fourth aspect of this typology: for there also exists a behavior of resignation which in the end leads to absorption, or indeed to liquidation.

The point of departure of an attitude of resignation is usually a monopoly situation that yields significant profit, with the underlying attitude that this income will continue to come in indefinitely thanks to a stable regulatory framework and economy. Supposed continuity of customer behavior, protection from external threats often ensured by the public authorities, a false sense of invulnerability linked to the large amount of resources accumulated by previous generations help explain this. A mind-set develops over a long period of time and results in the decision to live off former gains without challenging existing management practices, value systems, structures, and decision-making processes. Within this closed system, perpetuating the way in which the bank operates is the one aim of most senior managers. It is not held necessary to analyze competition or the environment and its evolution, for the strength of the past enables them to distance themselves from an outside world which seems to change only slowly. The consistent profitability of certain components of the bank acts as a shock absorber, enabling inevitable internal transformations to be put off.

These are precisely the underlying forces which deep down determine the behavior of certain institutions. One of the most spectacular examples of this mentality was the decision by a large bank to invest nearly half its capital outside its frontiers at a time when marketing and IT transformations, and the need to participate in and support domestic reindustrialization, demanded equal capital outlays. This kind of decision is far-reaching. Rather than upsetting working habits and culture, it appeared preferable to attempt to create significant profits from abroad, which in the best of hypotheses would avoid having to make necessary internal changes and in the worst of hypotheses would postpone the moment of having to do so.

But the facts are stubborn. To remain endlessly opposed to change is folly, as Bernard Shaw said when he wrote that the crazy man was he who adapted the world to his ideas; and to refuse to anticipate the transformations is an even more obvious folly.

Resignation is more than giving up the fight. It is tantamount to abandoning a certain ethic, a system of values based on professionalism and social responsibility. Analysis of the fundamental forces which lead a quality institution to adopt a position of resignation reveals that external changes are catalysts rather than determining factors. The absence of a group strategic intent, the refusal to apprehend a changing environment and to trigger off an internal dynamic process of change, are the real reasons for this abandonment. The blame does not lie with any specific decisions, but with a mentality that ignores the process of self-regeneration, which enables an institution to move from where it is back to a position of pre-eminence.

STRATEGIES OF CONQUEST

An offensive strategy is the expression of a powerful embodied vision maintained over time. It can only be adopted by a limited number of institutions and requires real will to succeed: for, as Balzac points out, "there is no great talent without great will." This spirit must be shared by the board of directors, the public authorities, and senior management, who will have to decide and to promote strategic orientations. This *de facto* support requires involvement which goes far beyond monthly or quarterly board meetings. We need external meetings once or twice a year, for two or three days at a time, during which the major orientations in business and sectoral policies are given full attention. The executive management of the Union des Banques Suisses, Citicorp, Fuji, and the Deutsche Bank meet in this fashion at regular intervals with their board of directors, who are usually chosen because of their complementary qualifications.

The board's composition is an important asset in the making and implementing of this type of strategy. It is made up of executives who have been successful in carrying out turnaround or expansion strategies in priority areas (the United States,

Europe, the Far East) or who have resounding victories to their credit in marketing policy in the large-scale distribution sector, information technology, or human resources and communication. Their contribution is measured not by participation in some prestigious round table but by their personal commitment to mobilizing experience and contacts.

An offensive strategy presupposes total commitment by the executive committee, which must reconcile two apparently contradictory requirements: diversity of temperament and experience and homogeneity in behavior and action. Refusal to take advantage of a diversity of talents is not compatible with an offensive strategy. But effective action also means coherency, an osmotic relationship between executives which is not achieved by chance but results from learning over a sustained period of time to work together toward the conquest of a market at world level. And this strategic intent must permeate the entire firm. The dichotomy between thinkers and players will become blurred, as it is poorly adapted to the requirements of present-day competition. Senior officials must give top priority to every employee in the organization, fostering their energy, their initiative, their ability to assume responsibilities, to take control of and supervise projects to the benefit of a common end. Shared determination, enshrined in this voluntarist framework expressed in various forms at every level of the organization, is a necessary condition for the deployment of an offensive strategy. But it can only find expression in tangible achievements over a sustained period of time. There are several reasons for this.

Tomorrow's bank will require a multitude of skills subject to rapid changes, whose mastery requires a long period of apprenticeship. (It is interesting to note in this regard a direct link between the reduction in or even elimination of certain training courses by large institutions in risk analysis or information technology, and the relative decline of these firms some ten years later. Such was the case of large houses like the Bank of America and Chase Manhattan.) The lure of immediate financial gains which encourage some of the best-performing managers, indeed entire teams, to switch institutions at huge "transfer" fees, together with the importance given to short-term results and individual performance are aspects of mentalities which need to be set on a new track. Unfortunately, the lasting acquisition of new values cannot be achieved overnight.

Let us suppose that the prerequisite for any strategy of conquest, that is, the strategic intent to become predominant in several activities in the domestic market, has been fulfilled. The first, but not necessarily the most important, target of an offensive strategy is the individual sector, the privileged area of application of a financial product policy that is bound to play a decisive role over decades to come in the profitability of banks and their power of intervention, and which allows access to the hard core of savings, the raw material of banking.

Not only do individuals provide the bank with stable deposits, they also represent a semi-captive market for a whole range of new services and investment products, financial or real estate assets. Furthermore, individuals contract debts in the form of consumer credit, mortgage credit, etc. This kind of business is particularly attractive to banks at a time when declining investment, the shrinking margins of many global firms and their direct access to other sources of capital, have led to a considerable reduction in the demand for and profitability of traditional commercial loans.

The second target of an offensive banking strategy is the corporate sector, which is vital in terms of both the national interests of the bank's home country and potential for long-term growth.

In this respect, the bank is like any other enterprise. Its *raison d'être* is to participate in the creation of a flow of national or international wealth. It is at the heart of the industrial firm that the mentalities and techniques which produce real wealth are shaped.

There is a striking correspondence between the emergence of the industrial powers and that of banks of world status: look at the United Kingdom up until 1930, the United States, France, and West Germany after World War II, Japan these past fifteen years. The reasons for this parallel development are numerous. The growth of diversified, long-standing industrial companies in an expanding economy has a multiplying effect on all a bank's activities. Industrial customer development, both domestic and international, which at times can reach an annual 10–20 percent growth rate, irrigates the entire banking infrastructure. Better still, daily work and osmotic relationships with industrial customers are conducive to behavior which generates wealth for the bank. Banks which have given priority to this market segment have come to introduce industrial management methods, which may involve work organization, long-term planning, or the adoption of new marketing or data-processing techniques. The stringent demands and tougher attitudes of the industrial customer "infect" the bank, bringing about a qualitative improvement in the banking service. This osmosis is often accelerated by transfers of people, and therefore of experience, at all levels.

The third sector of activity essential to a strategy of conquest is that of trading activities. This one differs from the two others on numerous counts. First of all, it is probably the only area of banking which is essentially global. The interlinking of the principal financial markets and interaction between the different products – from interest rates to stock market indices, from exchange rates to commodity markets, from futures in Chicago, London, or Paris to prime real estate – mean that access to information and expertise on a world scale is essential if maximum gains are to be made in a zero-sum game. This activity has to be performed where possible in real time, bringing into play considerable sums and advanced technologies. Pre-eminence in market activities is measured less in terms of volume and market shares, although for certain specialized products these are significant, than in the ability to co-ordinate, to control, and to gain the trust of very high-performing teams who must meet the increasingly exacting standards of corporate customers. One of the difficulties lies in persuading the banks to accept a system of management which must be differentiated. The working habits of the different market operators will vary widely according to the products they handled and the financial markets on which they work. The volumes at stake, the extent of fluctuations and therefore potential profits and losses, the rapid obsolescence of expertise (illustrated by the fact that an essential element of know-how these past few years has become the mastery of quantitative techniques) are all phenomena which explain the fragility of these teams, which seem in the West to form and disband at an alarming rate. If a bank is to hold on to the top trading teams who can bring it success, it will need not simply to hoist salaries higher and higher, but to effect a complete transformation of mentalities and thinking patterns. First of all, responsibility for securities trading activities must be entrusted to people endowed with a high level of both expertise and human sensitivity, who are capable both of devoting enough attention to each individual and simultaneously providing the trading room with trend guidelines and relieving operators of most of the administrative tasks. The model here should be that of a sports coach to a highly competitive team: someone capable of stimulating group spirit while at the same time encouraging individual performance.

This attitude is certainly indispensable in implementing a flexible and competitive profit-sharing system. Given the possibility of considerable individual gains available to market operators, it is essential to select those individuals on the basis of both technical and moral qualities, and to explain clearly to the entire management staff the reasons for differences in salaries, introducing wherever justified specific profit-sharing formulas related to the nature of the activity, while at the same time articulating them within an overall system which links them to the bank's overall results.

Profit-sharing is necessary, but, furthermore, a considerable amount of time and effort must be devoted to immersing the teams in a company spirit through meetings with the senior management, so that they identify themselves with the bank's values. The Union des Banques Suisses, which has practiced this method for well over twenty years now, has lost hardly any of its executives, despite the fact that quality traders in Switzerland are at a premium on the market. The same cannot be said of the large merchant or commercial banks in the United States and United Kingdom, which, favoring an almost exclusively financial approach, have often experienced large-scale defections.

An offensive strategy is clearly a very demanding one. It presupposes a solid base in the country of origin: the example of the Standard & Chartered Bank bears witness to the dangers of a narrow domestic base, which in the long run inevitably results in a shaky bank. However, experience shows that a pre-eminent position in the country of origin is a necessary but not a sufficient condition. The key to success resides for the most part in the elaboration and implementation of a strategy on a global scale, based on policies for human resources, information technology, and equity designed in an integrated fashion according to a long-term vision.

For French, British, or German banks, this means capturing over the next fifteen years significant positions or market share within the EC: otherwise they will no longer be able to lay claim to a world role; their target must be to tap a sizeable share of European savings and establish privileged relations with a large part of Europe's industrial and commercial companies. Considering the accelerating pace of concentration in American banking and the increased power of Japan's twenty leading banks, most of the banking institutions of the major European countries will probably in the next fifteen years become at world scale what regional banks are today at national level, in terms of captive deposits, privileged access to a clientele of individuals and companies, and capital supplies available to intervene in the field of trading or financing major projects or acquisitions.

Of course, size is not in itself a guarantee that a bank will remain in the front line and successfully carry out a strategy of conquest. The adverse effects of such well-known phenomena as bureaucratization and ossification can diminish the ability of a large bank to adapt to a market. However, size can procure room for maneuver in terms of the power of intervention and the ability to make investments whose results appear only over time, sometimes after more than a decade. Banking is a very capital-intensive activity and because of this it is slow to change. The absolute amount of real net assets, especially if they are used judiciously, therefore constitutes a sizeable comparative advantage. For reasons having to do with regulations, culture, and general policy, few of Europe's large banks have capital resources and a network on the scale of the European market. The 1992 deadline, the growing importance of intra-European trade, the transformation of mentalities symbolized by the role of the ECU and the increase in the number of European industrial poles all argue in favor of the creation of banking groups on a continental scale.

Several steps toward the achievement of this first stage can be envisaged. One of them consists in favoring endogenous growth. This is a policy systematically pursued by the Japanese banks, which have been patiently weaving a world network from a highly structured South-east Asian base. To do this, they rely on a managerial staff with three main characteristics: intimate knowledge of the group from which it descends; a moderate level of technical knowledge; and broad familiarization with the culture and working methods of the country where they have chosen to establish themselves. The policy of the Sanwa Bank, Japan's fifth largest, is significant in this respect. In 1978 it took the decision to establish itself in France at the beginning of the 1990s. In the course of implementing this plan it has every year sent two managers and their families to live in France for a period of two years, the first year being devoted to studying the banking business and the second year to becoming acquainted with French culture and working methods. The financial investment will not be made until the end of the period, after a long maturing process which will have endowed a sufficient number of quality managers with direct knowledge of the country.

In contrast, American banks, in particular Citicorp and, to a lesser degree, Chase Manhattan, have opted for a policy of multiform operations throughout the United States. Beginning in 1975, priority went first to recapturing the domestic market and then to the formation in the major states of multidisciplinary teams; Citicorp managed to make a remarkable breakthrough with the personal banking market. Chase and Citicorp enlarged considerably the range of products offered to companies: risk capital, cash management, consulting services on diversification and information technology. In parallel to this, acquisitions were made in the sectors of consumer credit, mortgage credit, credit cards, and insurance.

It is not certain that endogenous growth on a European continental scale is a serious option for the principal European banks. The extension to the EC of a domestic network does not appear very realistic considering the competition, the capital to be invested, and the reservoir of human talent that would be required. For the European banks, the global imperative probably takes the form of a mixed policy of endogenous growth and closer relations, acquisitions, or mergers, between institutions set up within the EC, at rates and terms suited to each case.

Two approaches are possible here: an integrated approach or a portfolio strategy. The first possibility takes into consideration a fact of experience: in banking any takeover or merger can save on time but not on human resources. How successful the growth-by-absorption option turns out to be depends on the quality of the assimilation process. Success requires a sufficient number of top-rate individuals to be detached who are capable of playing a key role across several company cultures and markets. The continuity and professionalism of those involved, the flexibility of management methods and of the decision-making process, and time will all be determining factors.

Dominance through financial investment is at first glance less demanding in terms of people and company cultures. But, as illustrated by the Crocker case, a closer look reveals risks which are not to be underestimated. This case was characterized by a lack of the financial controls that enable management to determine whether local expansion policies are justified; a loss of motivation and long-term commitment on the part of the most dynamic executives; difficulties in enabling the subsidiary to benefit from progress made by the parent company in organization, marketing, or technology.

The financial control lever is an often necessary but rarely sufficient condition for bringing about change in behavior and policies. The quality and number of the executive officers, the worth of the project which they embody and their working methods will all determine to what extent financially acquired institutions are likely to disappear or, on the contrary, to undergo renewed development. The example of Hongkong & Shanghai in the United States up until recently underlined the dangers and limits of the option of financial dominance.

There will be several difficulties in forming a European group, all tracing back to the fact that for several decades now most of the large banks have conducted their business within a framework more protected than that of industrial companies. Moreover, the considerable growth over the past ten years of the proportion of the net profits accounted for by the profitability of domestic activities has diminished the propensity to develop a strategy reaching beyond the national territory. Most of these institutions created a low-density foreign network which in general meets part of the international needs of their domestic customers. The only reason to modify a policy begun more than forty years ago is the changes imminent in the banking environment: for the regulations which partition European banking will be largely eliminated in 1992.

Furthermore, under the pressure of competition from the Far East, the United States, and some developing countries such as India and Brazil, interpenetration between European economies is bound to accelerate, with the creation in the end of a unified financial market destined to act as a catalyst to the integration of banking. Finally, the number and financial means of individuals – students, tourists, businessmen, self-employed workers, wealthy European individuals – wanting to benefit from a homogeneous service throughout Europe will necessarily increase in the next decade. Uniform services cannot be provided to these different customers by simple co-operation agreements, regardless of the degree of personal involvement by the managers of the institutions concerned. This course was fully explored within the EBIC, which for more than fifteen years now has organized meetings of hundreds of European managers with tangible, if modest, results. However, unity of purpose and accountability remains indispensable for meeting the triple challenge of foreign competition, incursions by industrial groups in the banking business, and new customer demands in the area of services and new products. Without this unity, the risk of failure increases, as was the case for most of the EBIC's subsidiaries, particularly outside Europe.

Is linking up with a European bank network the only solution available to an institution seeking to equip itself with the necessary means to outperform competitors in meeting expectations of a diversified clientele?

Another possible scenario is to join forces with an insurance group. The nature of its financial flows afford the insurance company funds available for long-term uses, while some of the bank's customers suffer from a lack of permanent resources. Under these conditions, is it conceivable that a banking group with teams particularly qualified to advise and to support an insurance firm in the development and diversification of its activities would form such an association to benefit from the other party's access to long-term funds? Complementary approaches can generate added value. Such an association, combining the insurance company's abilities to make long-term commitments and the bank's commitment to industry, is one way of solving the real problems many firms are finding in implementing their growth strategies. Nor are the effects induced insignificant for either the insurance company or the bank: complementary assessment of risk and enlargement of the customer base, at the cost of immense organizational and behavioral change in order to put these advantages to full use.

The interest of such an association is just as important for market activities. Insurance companies manage a considerable volume of liquidity which they invest first in their home market but with a growing tendency to diversify the geographical spread of both financial and real estate assets.

The level of experience and expertise of the large banks in trading and arbitrage between the world's different financial assets is generally much higher than that of the principal insurance companies. Banks in general employ higher quality traders and have better trading management support systems than most insurance companies. In the banks, the percentage of volume handled on their own account or for the account of a captive clientele is relatively low, whereas this type of transaction constitutes a determining factor of power and profitability in money-market activities. In this sector, properly organized relations between a bank and an insurance company can create a real competitive advantage.

At present, banks sell life insurance to individuals while insurance companies offer savings and pension products. All are aware that in the short and medium term, individual customers form the most profitable business segment. So banks have sought to increase market penetration in order to improve profitability through better depreciation of an important fixed cost, that is, a distribution network consisting of counters, branches, or general agents. It is therefore urgent that we create conditions favorable to collaboration. The task is complex, though, and involves redefining the role of each protagonist and the networks' mission and specialization. There is a long and exacting learning process here, requiring continuity and including numerous intermediary steps such as, possibly, the creation within the bank of an insurance sector and within the insurance companies of a banking activity.

In a strategy of conquest, the international financial markets have an important role to play. Only a limited number of institutions can take global judgments on anything concerning the trading of financial assets. Certain Japanese banks send their traders abroad with a double mission: that of taking advantage, within certain (often quite restrictive) limits, of the opportunities for arbitrage on the foreign market where they operate, and that of providing the head office with information enabling it to adopt appropriate positions, exploiting intervals between rising and falling cycles on the principal markets.

In this way Japan's leading banks move like a tidal wave from one market to the next, selling in New York only to invest then in London, Paris, Frankfurt. The financial assets and prime real estate market is managed in an integrated fashion. Investments run to billions of dollars. Such an approach, backed up by macroeconomic and microeconomic information of outstanding quality and by close relations between the head office and the overseas teams, offers opportunities for considerable gains and allows better use of fixed costs in investments in exchange rooms and by operators on these markets.

The market activities sector must, moreover, be a privileged medium for foreign investors wanting to buy financial or real estate assets in the bank's country of origin. Such is the role successfully played by the Deutsche Bank in Tokyo, where it meets the needs of Japanese investors in deutschmark assets. The leading French banks, in particular the Société Générale and Paribas, operate similarly. This volume of business can be highly profitable, as has been the case with financial flows originating in Japan and arriving in the United States and, more recently, with the United Kingdom and Europe, which has irrigated all the market activities of the principal American, British, and European merchant and commercial banks.

Money-market activities justify for a European bank a large presence in the United States and the Far East. The timeliness of a comparable move in the individual sector requires close examination.

The only bank of world status which has so far displayed a global strategy in the personal banking sector is Citicorp. The cultural factor is such a difficult element to overcome that results have been mixed so far in Europe; there was success in West Germany with the acquisition under excellent conditions of a consumer credit company (KKB) set up quite a few years back by the Germans and managed by them in exemplary and autonomous fashion, but the strategy has been less convincing in the United Kingdom and in France.

In the corporate finance sector, the creation of an international tool confers an unquestionable competitive advantage. It is worth noting the attempts made in this area by the leading British and American banks with the setting-up or repurchase of merchant banks or stockbrokers operating on the principal European markets in New York and in Tokyo. Experience demonstrates that the risks of this approach lie in the difficulty of developing trusting collaborative relationships among often independent teams within a large organization. Sustainable success is more likely to be achieved if senior management has already been successful in similar ventures at home, and has reconciled contrasting temperaments and approaches as well as different methods of remuneration under the same roof.

A strategy of conquest which combines power and flexibility is well suited to the demands of a world-level bank's customers. The whole art lies in carrying out such a project on one's own territory. This means careful choice of the people who will be responsible for leading the change, organizing co-ordination and communication between the different units, and defining decision-making methods. The approach required is simple. The bank's culture must recognize that the main investment is in human resources. Their recruitment, their training, the winning of their loyalty, and their appointment to positions which make the most of their potential and qualifications must not only be the focus of attention of senior executives but should take a large part of their time.

A survey conducted by the Midland Bank in 1979 of fifty large industrial firms which had remained leaders in their field for at least fifty years revealed that these different companies shared a single common denominator – their top executives devoted more than half their time to the firm's human resources and strategy. For there is an intimate link between durable financial success, human resource management, and strategic direction.

From 1950 to 1970 the entire executive committee of the Chase Manhattan Bank, from the chief executive officer to division heads, became accustomed to participating personally in the selection of each one of the 150 graduates annually appointed from America's top-ranking universities. Each of these new recruits was then followed for a period of two years by one of the senior executives, who devoted at least one hour a month to their protégé. These meetings provided the newcomers with the opportunity to discuss the general running of the bank with men of experience, and to share observations which they might have concerning their time in the various departments. In this way the trainees were directly exposed very early on in their working life to a system of values and to a general policy framework, while for their mentors listening to the concerns and aspirations of the young graduates was a source of enrichment for themselves as well as enabling them to guide the development and evaluate the potential of the next generation.

Around 1970, this system fell into disuse. It was considered too time-consuming. It followed that training ties and transmission of values and experience slackened, along with everything that implied in terms of loss of experience and know-how. Training and recruitment staff gradually replaced the role played by the operational head and the number of management training seminars was stepped up. Up until the end of the 1960s management stability had been one of this leading bank's strong points. Thereafter, resignations began to come in at an ever faster pace, after ten years reaching two-thirds of a year's intake of graduates. Between 1970 and 1989 Chase Manhattan fell from third place in the world's leading banks to number forty-two. The reasons for this decline are many; but the importance of the human factor must not be underestimated.

Recruiting, training, and gaining the loyalty of quality men and women is the first step; the bank must then go beyond this to elaborate a development plan which expresses its strategic intent. This is a normative rather than a descriptive approach and more clearly defines the firm's future, giving meaning to the daily work of each member of staff. Participation by the principal executives, indeed by the unions, as is now the case in some British companies, in the development of the company's strategy not only enhances it but triggers off an internal dynamic which encourages collaboration. At a time when job security cannot be taken for granted by executives, identification with a promising project is important to them, just as the implementation of flexible structures, modular rather than pyramid-shaped, conditions the move from strategy to action.

Managing this diversity while maintaining the unity of purpose and culture is one of the main challenges of implementing a strategy of conquest.

STRATEGIES OF CHANGE

Banks are like living organisms. They evolve in cycles and in certain periods of their development undergo phases of rupture which impose changes of direction and make survival their central preoccupation. Their tactics at these times are driven by a strategy of change.

For large institutions, while the crisis may appear sudden to the outside world, there will have been numerous signs within the bank that foreshadow the event: financial losses, decline of market share, key personnel departure, inability to position itself successfully in new markets. What is really at stake for an institution facing this type of situation is the need to protect the essential part of its living substance until it can once again find and promote a project with a promising future, having brought to light the reasons for the decline and determined the new constraints within which the bank must redefine its purpose and mission.

The causes of the essential problems encountered by the large banking institutions are many. The most profound is the one that it wants most of all to avoid – the mismatch of the bank's existing culture and its major strategy. Toward the end of the 1970s, for instance, the Bank of America decided to invest nearly $1 bn in restructuring its entire information technology infrastructure. At that time the financial constraint seemed so easy to control that the most advanced software and computers were chosen. The results soon dampened ambitions. Unfortunately, the bank did not perform enough market segment analyses to define and control its relations with the environment. Macroeconomic studies consisted largely in extrapolating previous years' trends; they did not perceive that changes in the domestic market, in particular on the west coast of the United States, risked turning a position of strength into one of weakness. Increased industrial and agricultural risks had not been taken into account, while Security Pacific had already taken the necessary precautionary steps. Furthermore, advanced technologies were chosen without any previous correct assessment of the organization's ability to make a qualitative and quantitative jump of this kind. The result was that, just when the firm's net margin was burdened with bad debts because of a fall in the quality of traditional assets, overhead rose sharply; but it was not matched by a reduction in costs by the elimination of repetitive tasks, nor was there an improvement in the quality of customer service.

Bureaucratic management of human resources, a long-term plan centralized in the hands of a few specialists, a narrow approach to budgetary control, partitioning of departments, and pyramid-shaped decision-making structures are just some of the characteristics of a company culture which led to the sharp decline of one of the world's leading banks, which during the first two decades after World War II had been content with managing what it had so brilliantly achieved.

All the large banks that have undergone this experience have a trait in common: their principal orientations were not decided after patient analysis and transformation of the organization, with a group of individuals committing themselves to learning new ways and evolving in order to complete a project successfully. Instead, decisions were made mainly on the basis of how they would affect the bank financially, that is to say, with the idea that they would reduce the parameters to be reconciled, illustrating a form of magical solution: that money can solve all problems. Any change in strategy is by definition multidimensional and requires, in order to be successful, a thorough change in mentality.

The first motive of a strategy is survival. In the case of a bank, more than any other enterprise, this imperative stems from the priority given to measures to re-establish basic financial equilibrium. Time is money and it is important to devise and implement the reorganization plan both without delay and also as a whole project whose coherence reflects senior management's control of events. A traditional recovery plan generally includes sale of assets, replenishment of equity, and elimination of unprofitable sectors in which it does not appear possible to acquire a lasting competitive advantage in the short or medium term.

At this stage, the objective is clear. The aim is to recover a certain freedom of maneuver, to recreate a range of opportunities. The implications are necessarily financial. Thus the Dresdner Bank and the Commerzbank at the beginning of the

1980s decided to sell off industrial investments, to remodel their money-market activities, and to adjust their dividend policy in order to replenish equity through self-financing. As for the Bank of America, it chose a different course. It sold off some of its best assets to various buyers and reduced overhead significantly without being able to identify a guiding principle or long-term prospects. Nevertheless, financial results have been encouraging in 1989/90.

This necessary first phase recreates a space within which the plan can be deployed. It is a crucial time in the life of a company. The double meaning of crisis as both danger and opportunity must be used as a springboard to the future. At this stage a movement must be generated, and this can only occur from within. Every community is driven by a need for security and a need for identification: these act in symbiosis, one capable of compensating the other. In time of crisis, security inevitably diminishes and an equilibrium can only be maintained by reinforcing a sense of identification with the strategy; the staff will be more willing to assume a greater risk if they have a clear perception of the direction chosen and the nature of the challenge facing them.

Having acknowledged the importance of internal motivation, a vast research and analysis project must be set in motion to establish, with sufficient precision to protect the figures from internal challenge, the contribution of each sector of activity to profits and to generate a list for each one of them of the key factors of success. This is followed by a study of the environment and its evolution.

Beyond published figures and documents, it is helpful if senior executives are in direct contact with customers so that they may be attuned to their needs. Face-to-face encounters with all kinds of clients in order to determine the added value that the bank can provide, are a complementary option to the hiring of outside consultants to do a market study.

Taking account of competitive conditions is an essential step. Executives have everything to gain from dialogue with their counterparts. This was the road taken by Jaguar's chief executive officer when he had to reorganize a desperate financial and industrial situation. One of his first decisions was to spend several days at Mercedes and thoroughly study how the firm's research department was organized and what its manufacturing method and marketing policy were.

A change in strategy means immersion in a new standard and the definition of a new qualitative point of reference. Acute and precise awareness of the real constraints facing the firm is also necessary. The easy way out is to overestimate the lack of capital. By placing too much importance on this factor, a justification is found for ignoring other reforms which are much more difficult to implement. In the area we are examining, this is seldom the case. Capital exists in abundance. What is of the utmost importance are the financial ratios. The market anticipates a certain level of earnings per share and it is up to each sector to determine the outlook on profitability in relation to the amount of capital expenditure or operating costs that it would like to see itself allocated. Moreover, the supervisory bodies have their requirements for balancing large balance-sheet amounts, expressed by a series of ratios. For a bank, as for most companies which have reached a certain degree of maturity, the financial dimension should only be used as a yardstick to measures performance over time. Generally speaking, it is no longer a scarcity factor and it could not in any case be the core of a strategy.

The most important part of a change in strategy is refocusing on activities where the firm traditionally excels. For a large bank, the point of departure is still its branch network. Formed over several decades, it is the human skeleton of a bank, a breeding ground for executives who have learned to command in the field, and the means of capturing a pool of customers. This potential must now be used in a different and better way by drawing on marketing and IT to promote a new range of products and services. The bank's traditional sectors must also be reinforced; it must retain this competitive edge and ensure that it remains in step with customer trends.

There are several factors which strongly favor a strategy founded on a bank's strong points. First of all, there is generally high profitability and particularly close customer relations. If this can be exploited, new profit flows can be raised rapidly. This was the option taken up by the Commerzbank, whose centers of excellence included fund management, relations with medium-sized companies, and a particularly successful presence in certain regions of West Germany. The Dresdner Bank followed the same path, favoring large corporate accounts, industrial investments, certain selected segments of money-market activities, and a few direct presences abroad. Midland decided to concentrate its efforts on individuals, small and medium-sized companies, Thomas Cook travel packages and travelers' checks, and on developing certain offices in foreign countries where they had a particularly favorable position, such as West Germany, France, and Switzerland.

Although this approach has the definite advantage of attending to the most urgent things first, it does not fall within the framework of a global approach that can mobilize all a bank's resources. Such an approach presupposes a system of reference on the basis of which each bank can define itself. As soon as a bank begins to encounter difficulties, it must plan its recovery by integrating two dimensions: an overall approach and a set of specific measures. The first aspect is crucial and involves redefining precisely the bank's mission, clearly explaining its purpose and ensuring the entire staff's acceptance through a process of consultation and thorough communication.

The significance of this is illustrated by the answer to one simple question: does the bank want to maintain its independence or not? If it really does, commitment to its autonomy can be enough to create a powerful current of motivation and thus to generate a culture which will make it possible to implement difficult decisions.

Interiorization of the process of recovery is often considered superfluous and treated with skepticism, even derision. However, examination of what truly motivates enduringly successful industrial or financial undertakings strikingly reveals the extreme importance that executives attach to this aspect of their firm's life. Morgan Guaranty Trust, the Deutsche Bank, and the Industrial Bank of Japan have all been able to develop a clear and coherent vision of their mission. In the framework of a strategy of complete change, this is the most important task. There is no substitute for it.

The process described above will help define a new orientation. Can the reorganized bank that emerges after the crisis continue to exist as such? What risks does it run if the last few years' performances and operations are extrapolated? In what form does it intend to be present in the sectors or market segments that have been given priority? This internal investigation brings out into the open the many sides of the risks assumed and defines what has to be done today and in the near future if long-term success is to be achieved. Acute awareness of the challenges and dangers facing the bank is essential to clear decision making and to sustaining the will to succeed.

The first short-term decision for a large branch network should be to favor mass processing. We live in a time of unprecedented growth in the volume of financial operations, largely because of the interest shown by small and medium-sized depositors in increasingly diversified and sophisticated assets and financial products, and the exponential growth of money-market activities. In this environment, the demand for a reliable and consistent service continues to grow. A high and stable level of profitability can be generated if the bank has managed to introduce simultaneously information technology which judiciously combines microcomputers and big systems alongside human resource management methods based on industry: namely, development of procedures and software which increase quality, from the design and pilot phases onwards.

Experience has shown that, if managed differently, most of a bank's traditional activities can be very profitable. These must now be prioritized; during a bank's phase of decline, the tendency is to treat them like a poor relation, being niggardly in granting financial and human resources, while spending lavishly on innovative and spectacular activities.

Another decision should be to phase out specific existing products which have been insufficiently developed: wide-scale dissemination of money products or real estate assets is an example of this.

Finally, in the corporate sector the bank must choose

specialties where it intends to dominate. The Midland Bank decided on sterling options, international trade financing, maritime freight, and aircraft financing; Chase Manhattan Bank chose, among other things, to protect its market share in the oil and electronics industries. These business choices must be implemented in light of the bank's profitability constraint; overheads can be 15 per cent to 30 percent higher than those of the best placed competitors.

Reduced costs and innovation are intimately linked simply because a light structure favors the emergence of new ideas. It is easier to develop innovative banking products and services in a context of decentralization where relatively small units can experiment with new ideas. These germinate in the field, are tested locally, and, if results are positive, are adopted throughout the company. At the Midland Bank, for example, a group of branches joined forces to develop homemade telecommunications modules in real time for local small and medium-sized firms. This successful experiment was then extended to the entire network. It was directly tied in with money-market activities, which made it possible to reach a group of customers hitherto untapped and to offer them a highly profitable and competitive service.

This case is a good illustration of a likely development among banks, with a number of profit-generating, innovative concepts emanating from small groups in direct contact with day-to-day customer needs. Flexible and decentralized structures help disseminate these initiatives. This method is an integral part of the development process of the large Japanese banks and explains how they were able, after long periods of incubation and apparent opposition to change, to make qualitative and quantitative improvements that the outside world was surprised to see rapidly executed by an entire group.

However, defining a mission and making business decisions are only first steps, not ends in themselves. Everyone knows that no decision has ever changed reality; only its implementation does that. Therefore, concrete medium-term objectives should be defined for each of the large sectors which make up the framework of the banking institution, with particular emphasis on the fact that the difficulty consists not in determining whether the market exists but how to handle it. A practical means of implementation, which was experimented with successfully at the Midland Bank, is to divide up each large department into autonomous profit centers: that is, units which in theory could each be dealing with a relatively homogeneous group of customers to whom it offers specific services. Each unit could have its own operating account. The profit centers are classified in order of importance, and the needs in terms of investment and overhead allocation are added up. Most of the bank's investment is in human resources: development of a particular sector is ensured by appropriation of an autonomous and sufficient overall budget. As is frequently the case, in particular in a bank which has undergone a major shock, the demand for financial resources will exceed what is available: hence the need for arbitration.

Employing a modular structure, trimming of central services, use of simplified management information, choice of executives capable of inducing changes in behavior, management by objectives, an internal and external communication policy – these are just some of the principal transformations to be made over a period of three to five years in order to implement successfully a strategy of change.

There will be numerous temptations to take short cuts, to do without the company strategy, to skip steps and contract alliances with other institutions which are also having certain difficulties, or even to adopt essentially financial solutions, such as merger in a holding company with other financial organizations, insurance companies, hire-purchase companies, or merchant banks. But though it may be possible to gain time financially with such an approach, it only puts off the moment when a bank is really capable of moving ahead by itself; for this movement can only be generated from within.

STRATEGIES OF CONSOLIDATION

Consolidation is an intermediate strategy relevant to three stages of a bank's development. First, it may precede a strategy of conquest, when it corresponds to a phase of accumulation. The bank becomes a depository for reserves in people, in culture, and in capital, indicating its desire to reach a critical mass whereupon everything is created, often according to an overall plan but sometimes in the course of hesitant experiments and guesswork.

Secondly, there is an indispensable phase of assimilation right after an offensive period during which the firm's human, technical, and financial resources have been fully deployed. This contrasts with the earlier stage of concentration. Changes in balance occur both in dealings with the outside world and in internal functioning, changes which must be assimilated if they are not to harm the bank's future development.

The third facet of consolidation is conservation. Enhancements are made sparingly, there is some touching up and some discarding. There is restoration. Whatever is new is scrutinized and only that which can be fitted into existing molds is incorporated.

These three facets of a strategy of consolidation certainly look like arbitrary cuts in a situation which is actually more complex and confusing than it would seem. But what is really important is that each of these phases has its own internal logic and corresponds to profound reorientations which transform the bank's financial base, the company plan, and the internal operating rules, and therefore its future.

In the years following World War II, after satisfying the most urgent requirements of reconstruction or development of their national economies, the large American, European, and Japanese banks underwent a period of consolidation. This maturing period preceded the expansion of international and then of money-market activities. Each bank took advantage of these years differently. It was during this incubating phase that operating methods were confirmed or amended. US banks developed their strategic plan and intent. For the next two decades these methods were to shape each institution's respective potential for development.

The first priority was meeting the financing needs of domestic industrial firms within the regulatory framework. In this context of widespread growth, recollections of the 1929 stock market crash had a particular influence on the United States, West Germany, and to a lesser extent France, when it came to elaborating banks' missions and systems of values. The emphasis in the United States fell on evaluating credit risk; the bank failures of the 1930s had so deeply marked members of the banking community that this became the cultural pivot of the large American banks. Controlling commercial risk became the keystone of a system of values with all that implied in terms of behavior and organization.

This meant that firms needed individuals who could understand the industrial and financial decisions of their customers. Recruitment methods had to be entirely transformed; the end of the 1950s saw the arrival of the first large contingents of graduates, between 100 and 150 recruits each year, who received two to three years of very extensive training. In order to maintain a minimum cultural common denominator within firms, the training centers created at this time also took in high flyers from other parts of the firm and who appeared to have particularly high potential. Throughout this period and in just one bank, over 2,000 executives were trained this way, using methods that had already been proven effective in industry. Chase Manhattan Bank and Citicorp frequently dispatched representatives to study recruitment and training practices at, among others, General Motors, Ford, and General Electric. A similar approach was adopted later by the large European and Japanese firms, often ten years behind the American banks, mainly because of the limited human and financial resources available at the time and also because of the different prevailing culture.

Against this background, the multiplicity of existing banks

took a variety of paths depending, on the one hand, on national legislation and temperament, and on the other hand, on reorientations decided on by their senior managements.

A closer relationship with industry led to various changes. Citicorp took a step that at the time was considered radical when it decided to apply more of industry's methods to banking. The organization of labor, cost price analysis, the notions of research laboratories, products, and marketing were all imported, with all that implied in terms of cultural upheavals. Along with the revolution in assessing the credit risk for companies, application of an industrial approach to the internal conduct of business was the decisive change which the large American banks underwent during this period of maturation.

The most radical transformation was unquestionably that made by Citicorp, to whom goes the credit for having put forward a new model. Immersed in an industrial vision of bank management, it forged an effective instrument in the course of the 1960s founded on a system of values, teams, and new working methods, having fulfilled the essential preliminary conditions for a strategy of conquest. This explains the spectacular results it has obtained over the past 15–20 years in personal banking, money market, and wholesale activities.

Chase Manhattan took a more restrained approach during this period, limiting itself for the most part to transforming its credit risk evaluation methods and creating its own reservoir of talent. Its management at that time did not want to adopt industrial methods in their entirety. Hence, it was unable to forge the tool suited to future requirements, and was accordingly penalized when it tried to position itself in the personal, international, and money markets.

The phase of consolidation can be defined as one in which the ability to act, that is, the ability to transform reality with the eventual creation of value-added services, is elaborated and developed. One particular aspect of this process deserves attention, because it has had such major repercussions on the entire world banking system. It is the case of loans to developing countries.

The large American banks, in particular Citicorp and Chase,

made their debut in this area in the 1950s by lending considerable sums to Japan which was then the developing country *par excellence*. The financial ratios of private borrowers at that time broke all the rules: the ratio between total debt and equity was frequently around 8:1. The risk evaluations made by the credit departments were confined to identifying the excessive level of debt and concluding that while the risk was impossible to assess, all things considered it was acceptable because it involved "Japan Inc." and a country could not go bankrupt. This analysis was reduced to its simplest expression. It included no in-depth study of Japan's industrial situation, the borrower's development strategy, or the contrast between its industrial strategies and those of major existing clients such as US Steel. Such pragmatism was beneficial in the short term. Because of high margins of 1.5–2 percent, Japan's activity represented for some banks up to 80 percent of profits from international lending.

Once the Japanese debt was repaid, the American banks sought other outlets – retaining similar methods of analysis.

From that time on, a double standard emerged: on the one hand, caution toward American, then European industrial firms, where they had an intimate knowledge of the economic and human environment, a detailed analysis of the industrial strategies, and influence over the use made of the capital committed; and blind trust of numerous developing countries purely on account of the success they had had with reconstruction loans to Japan. Habits of thought acquired during the period of consolidation persisted until recently, as witnessed by the survival of certain aphorisms such as "a country cannot go bankrupt" in the vocabulary of financial executives. In reality, however, the situation of many countries is similar to that of a state of suspension of payments.

This reference to Japan and to habits picked up during the reconstruction period is also evident in the priority accorded to short-term credits to developing countries, considered less risky than medium- or long-term financing. Indeed, reconstruction of Japan's steel industry was for the most part financed by six- or twelve-month loans renewed periodically. The same practice was adopted fifteen years later for Argentina, Mexico, and Brazil, when the absence of any real analysis by a few large banking institutions of how wealth is created and on a country's capacity to repay debt led some people to compare Argentina's risk favorably with that of Japan.

Between 1965 and 1980, a period which preceded the phase of conquest, the Japanese banks, like the American banks, prioritized the national industrial fabric. However, their approaches differed radically. In the course of these fifteen years, Japanese banks favored partnership with Japanese industry, and did not content themselves with half-measures. Like the American banks, the Japanese banks formed their own reservoir of graduates. However, such talent would for the most part be devoted to tasks that contributed directly to the development of each of the industrial and commercial companies which made up the bank's customer base. Hundreds of executives were dispatched to these companies and assigned to the financial, marketing, technical, or planning departments. In addition, the banks equipped themselves to perform macroeconomic analyses; to carry out studies of individual branches of industry; to undertake very detailed market surveys; to recruit engineers capable of evaluating foreign patents and the technological competitiveness of their customers. Moreover, the Japanese bankers were united in recognizing the importance of such an effort.

In fact, banking assistance, in all its forms represents but one aspect of the service in Japan. Most of the large banking institutions see the development of Japanese industry as the basis of their ethic. Everything is subordinate to it, even certain aspects of the bank's internal modernization.

Some are surprised at the low productivity of many of the big Japanese banking groups in contrast to their exceptional stock market performances. But the paradox is only apparent. In the course of these fifteen years of consolidation, and sometimes even before that, the large Japanese banks forged their own doctrine and spread it within their own institutions. The capture of international markets occurs in the wake of the capture of their own industry. Even today, the Fuji Bank in

London, with a balance-sheet total of more than £15 bn, makes over 80 percent of its profits from its Japanese customers. And cash surpluses cleared by the large Japanese companies have made them privileged players in the capital markets.

The current success of Japanese banks is clearly the fruit of their labors. Having given priority to investment in people and allocated most of their resources to modernization of the industrial base, Japan's banks can now benefit from the multiplying effect of the growth of their industrial customers. Loyalty to the banks is especially solid since they were able to create a network of contacts of unprecedented density, woven with persistence over several decades.

The contrasting approach of British commercial banks reveals major differences in national temperament. Up until recently, industry has been rather looked down upon by British banks, except for the financing of international trade where the London market has traditionally played a pre-eminent role. The reasons for his behavior are complex. For several decades now, the merchant banks have attracted some of the most talented individuals. This is not a neutral choice and reflects a very widespread feeling that industry is a somewhat ignoble activity, indeed, that it destroyed traditional values to which most of the country's leaders were attached. This prejudice, combined with an evident taste for gambling in all its forms, largely explains why finance found a receptive environment in Britain.

The activity of the large commercial banks focuses for the most part on two priorities, both lucrative: the development of personal banking, ranging from deposit collection to consumer credit, and intermediation activities. British commercial banks opened their doors to university graduates at a much slower rate than their American, Japanese, and even European counterparts. The banking services offered to industry are limited to a traditional range and there are few plans to extend them to include products which make a greater positive contribution to companies' operations. During the phase of consolidation between 1960 and 1980, priority was given to reinforcing profit margins and equity. The decision to favor capital formation had a determining effect on the methods selected during the phase of conquest. The financial approach was preferred by most of the intervening parties, who rejected the idea of developing industry or implementing management tools modeled on those adopted by the top-performing European, American, and Japanese banks. Large amounts of resources in the form of shareholders' equity and a particularly large financial market facilitated growth by acquisition or merger, both in Great Britain and abroad. Over the past fifteen to twenty years there has been an increase in the acquisition of merchant banks, exchange agents, stockbrokers, real estate networks, and travel agencies, and takeovers by foreign, in particular American, commercial banks.

The West German and French banks have opted for an intermediate course. Germany is the closer of the two to the Japanese experience, for close relationships between the German banking system and industry have their roots in a time-honored tradition. Beginning in the 1960s, the Deutsche Bank built up a large, talented, high-quality reservoir of men and women. It worked in the heart of industry at all levels: selection of directors, alignment, definition of development strategies, long-term financing. It devoted a sizeable share of its equity to investment in these companies and chose endogenous growth based on privileged relations with German industry. The French banks embarked on a course closer to their German counterparts than to the British, but their involvement in France's industrial fabric was generally on a considerably lesser scale. There were, nevertheless, similarities, particularly in the way industrial methods were gradually applied to the bank's internal management.

Each national system took advantage of this period of consolidation to reinforce its strengths. The strategy of consolidation corresponded to a phase where the banking institution sowed the seeds of its future.

However, there is another strategy of consolidation which satisfies a different imperative, namely, that of assimilating an expansion whose principal phases have just been completed. This is the second facet mentioned above. In this case, emphasis goes to reconstituting, if not a homogeneous, at least a coherent whole after a period in which the scope of activities has been enlarged in terms both of products and of geographical coverage. The problem is first and foremost a qualitative one. In essence, it can be formulated as the question of how to reconcile diversity in operating methods and in cultures with capitalizing on the strength associated with the mass effect of a large banking group of world status.

A number of simple rules can be formulated according to Montesquieu's maxim: "The same virtues which serve to found an empire serve also to keep it." First, the *clarity* of the strategy of conquest must be maintained. A look at the Union des Banques Suisses is relevant here. UBS focused its mission on service to industry and the adoption of internal management methods comparable to those of its principal customers. For over fifteen years now, in the heart of a training center opened in Worfsberg, UBS has set itself the objective of elaborating a philosophy of action which takes into account both future requirements and its traditional values. It chose a site whose architecture reflects both the bank's roots in a past reaching back over several centuries and its progress into the future. The training program is undergone by a large number of executives who attend for several months over a period of ten years. Its approach is multifold and includes a concern to develop the personality of each participant, an in-depth reflection on the decision-making process and its follow-up, a concrete search for a new balance between the demands of a polymorphous market which supposes a considerable delegation of authority to united teams, and the conviction that quality is synonymous with profitability. In an effort to capture new markets and to enlarge its range of activities, the UBS had to assimilate its executives, who were from various backgrounds, by providing them all with the same technical and leadership training. After much thought, it was decided that the seminars would be conducted in English, despite all the difficulties associated with that choice, for such problems were considered minor compared with the need to disseminate a philosophy of action from the home base which applied to executives of all nationalities.

Finally, we must address the third facet of the consolidation strategy: that which hovers on the border between two worlds, between resignation and renewal. We are concerned here with the period which follows a major setback; priority goes to conservation and reassertion. In this case, financial reorganization is necessarily the most important task. An equilibrium must be re-established in the balance sheet by creating, if possible, a margin for maneuver, for in this kind of consolidation strategy time plays a pivotal role. The passage of time allows the past to settle and procures the respite necessary before triggering off new action. Reinforcement of equity obtained from an increase of capital, sale of assets, and rationalization of management all make for a gap in time. How can this be turned to good account?

The main risk lies in weakening the bank's internal motivating forces, with the departure of the most able executives, a downgrading of image, and, from the point of view of the stock market, a fall in the price/earnings ratio. There must be a plan if this trend is to be reversed. Stopping the decline and, by so doing, protecting a bank's independence, constitutes a highly mobilizing goal. At this stage of a bank's life, the function of its chief executive officer is decisive. The CEO personifies an ambition. He or she plays the role of collector and disseminator of information; it is he or she who propels the most difficult changes in people, in culture, in behavior, and in business choices.

In this situation, the strategy of consolidation returns to basics, goes back to the bank's core. This has to be done quickly because uncertainty at a time of crisis is pernicious. Within the span of a few months, it is necessary that the essential outlines of tomorrow's bank are identified, that the decision-makers capable of bringing about the change are identified, and that the key teams whose mission it will be to implement the orientations selected are in place. Discernment and authority are therefore vital at such a time in order to lead the company into a virtuous circle where the process of wealth creation is once again triggered off.

◇

Conclusion

◆

Finance, and more particularly banking, has a place alongside technology as one of the essential means of mastering our economic future. The right to impact capital allocation, whether it involves equity or current liabilities, and control of the interface between consumers and suppliers of financial goods and services, affects not only the creation of wealth but also its distribution. An economic community, either on the national or the continental scale, which increasingly lags behind in the area of advanced industries with diminishing control over the financial space, suffers a severe handicap in terms of the evolution of both living standards and political influence.

The world banking scene is undergoing fundamental transformation. Future shock is here now, with the triple effect of the information-technology revolution, the emergence of the Japanese pole, and the regulatory changes. The effects of these three catalysts are increasingly perceptible; gradual evolution over a period of fifteen years or so does not appear very likely because the forces for change are so powerful. For those who know where they want to go and are determined to provide themselves with the means to get there, success is waiting.

For over a decade, large banking institutions in both Europe and the United States have given priority, on the one hand, to household accounts, consumer credit, and estate management, and on the other to money-market activities on the spot and forward markets, and the futures and options markets, supported by virtually paper-free systems. These operations account for more than fifty times the volume of international trade. They can ensure those banks capable of securing the best-performing teams a source of considerable income, both directly and through the effects induced on firms and individuals. But the money game at world level and the management of household needs, however lucrative, does not exhaust a large bank's *raison d'être*, just as deposit collection was not the only purpose of similar institutions until 1975. For more than a century, the transformation of current deposits into medium-and long-term credits to finance trade and industry constituted one of the fundamental reasons for the existence of banks. The banker, by assuming credit risks, played a pivotal role in the wealth-creation process.

The trends of the past decade and more have not eliminated the need for companies to find in a banker a privileged speaking partner. Rather, the nature of that need has changed. A bank's partnership with a firm now requires a high level of services and a selective commitment in equity. The bank continues to be an intermediary but the content of this intermediation is different. The bank's mission no longer consists primarily of lending over a long period of time deposits collected by its network, but in allocating as a matter of priority gains originating from other sectors, and in particular from speculation on the markets, to industrial development. Assistance to industrial and service companies must once again become *the central priority of bank development*.

This decision is binding. It requires the creation or development of a reservoir of expertise which can work in osmosis with the firms. It is necessary, moreover, to have the financial means to back the policy. Tomorrow's bank must find its way back on to the road to creating real wealth by allowing its industrial partners to benefit from its judgment and its knowledge of business, from its network of contacts, and from a privileged financial commitment that involves the bank in its customers' development without tipping over into interference.

However, this commitment cannot be limited to national territory, or even to a continent; it is a world scale commitment because the industrial challenge is clearly this big. Most industrial firms have experienced growth in three main geographical areas, according to their backgrounds: the European Community, North America, and South-East Asia. This growth has occurred in a gradual and variegated fashion:

through direct presence, partial or total acquisitions, trade and technology agreements, and joint ventures. Each of these courses is complex in terms of both conception and implementation. To explore them, to conclude successfully the negotiations specific to each one of them, and finally, to promote the growth of these units in their respective markets – all this requires a wide range of contacts and know-how.

Certainly an international industrial firm can orchestrate these different steps on its own by soliciting in sequence the banks which it believes best suited to the specific needs of each stage. However, experience shows that customized service of this kind has its limits. Its efficiency is low compared with the approach which consists of a firm joining up with a few banks of world status which have become intimately acquainted over the years with its management and their development strategies and are prepared once again to give priority to their customers' growth. If the people are qualified and experienced, the extent and duration of links between the two firms contributes decisively to the success of the wealth creation process. Relations of complementarity are established: thanks to its positioning, the bank is able to create development opportunities and to facilitate their implementation; in return, it benefits from diversified and significant financial flows. Industry and bank become long-term partners.

A permanent relationship based on reciprocal commitment stemming from an industrial project represents for the customer an asset which is more valuable than the provision of services that he can expect from an institution which conceives of its role essentially as that of a financial product supermarket.

The correlation, for nearly a century now in the United Kingdom and more recently in the United States, between a certain industrial decline and the idea that the banks had of their mission is worth noting. There probably exists, at least in part, a causal link on a scale which should not be underestimated. However, the bank which embarks on this course of industrial partnership as a line of priority strategic development, must provide itself with the means to back its policy by setting up, in the large industrial regions, stable and competent commercial teams which cover the world like a spider's web, and by making available capital resources appropriate to this sector's needs. Some will consider this a return to basics contrary to the spirit of the times. However, there is no alternative. This is the only approach that will generate lasting wealth for the whole of society. It guarantees, moreover, the bank's durability. By strengthening the customer base and by making a commitment to the promotion of industrial customers' growth, the bank triggers off a dynamic reaction of development which irrigates all its activities. Simultaneously, it distances itself from competition with non-bank enterprises which have recently stepped up their activities in consumer credit and the sale of financial products – areas hitherto reserved for the banks. Of course, the development of a banking culture which favors service and commitment to manufacturing and service industry requires internal education spread over several decades, while the entry of an automobile manufacturer or a supermarket chain with high quality IT on to the consumer credit market and the distribution of insurance or investment products to individuals can occur fairly quickly.

The Deutsche Bank long ago chose to become a catalyst of greater competitiveness among its industrial customers. Recently, it took control of one of the largest European consultancy firms and grouped together under the same management all its industrial investments and company credit activities. Furthermore, it spent almost $1 bn on buying the Bank of America's Italian banking network and close to $1 bn to gain control of Morgan Grenfell. In time it is likely to invest on a similar scale in other European countries and in the United States. Gradually, the Deutsche Bank has set up structures and a world organization consistent with its intentions, namely, to provide the corporate market segment with the range of services required to reinforce its competitiveness in the decades ahead without, however, neglecting its other priority, which is to become the dominant banking force in East Germany, where it plans to open 200–300 branches, and to be present in other selected East European countries.

Of course, there exist numerous models of development and

each large bank must generate internally its own strategy, taking into account its historical background and the general context in which it operates. Once the main orientations have been decided, the real challenge facing the bank's executives is to translate the vision which they have of its future into day to day decisions. This vision is characterized by the internationalization of competition, the extension of information, and the gradual reduction of hierarchical relationships. Everyone knows from experience that no decision has ever changed anything. Everything lies in the art of execution; and the best results in this area are obtained by organizations which have assimilated at all levels the processes which enable a project to take shape.

The first step consists in creating the movement. The organization must be placed under tension by assigning it credible objectives that motivate action and that are decided on the basis of wide consensus: for example, become the leading European bank or financial group, in terms of market share and profitability; contribute to the positioning of various segments of a domestic industry on a continental scale; serve as catalyst in the creation of a global banking group. All these examples illustrate what is at stake and what can mobilize a bank's vital forces. In order for it to develop, each company needs a strategy which mobilizes the entire organization and justifies the constraints which it imposes on itself. It must therefore have men and women in senior management positions who have the capacity to think with imagination, to anticipate, and to design with rigor an implementation process. Their role consists first in identifying market potentialities and in formulating global objectives.

Then, the strategic plan must be patiently shared with every level in the organization so that each individual understands the content and nature of his or her contribution. At this stage, there is no improvised action, but a great deal of meticulous work whereby each employee defines the existing gap between the current situation and the goal to be reached, clarifies the means necessary to achieve his or her own objectives, has access to a management system enabling him or her to measure results and determine the reliability of forecasts and, consequently, to adopt any necessary corrective or preventive measures. This approach is based on several considerations. It responds first of all to a concern for efficiency, in that constant interplay between a global vision and a targeted approach enables optimal use of company resources. A global vision is indispensable at a time when the increase in personal incentives risks making the firm a simple amalgam of individual adventures; and the desire to assume responsibilities and to be able to make decisions at one's own level of expertise are factors that determine a company's dynamism. At a time when the guiding values are company spirit, the ability to adapt, personal and team commitment, it is important to increase the responsibilities of all active employees, in particular by making traders, branch managers, and specialists contribute directly to the bank's strategy. They are in direct contact with a complex and changing commercial and technical reality; it is essential that they be put in a situation where, in the field, they can take advantage of opportunities and compensate for any shortcomings.

In order to achieve this result, it is often necessary to change company culture and individual behavior. Change cannot be decreed or improvised. It can be induced, provided that certain pitfalls are avoided. The temptation to let things run their own course, based on the conviction that changes occur for the most part by themselves, must be avoided. It is also necessary to get around pointillism, that is to say, piecemeal modification of certain elements of a general policy, such as the policy on communication, remuneration, or the introduction of microcomputers, without these measures being part of a coherent overall plan. Finally, the conditions for exercising authority must be changed. The bank must move away from a situation where the head office is omnipresent to a modular structure where only a few functions are centralized: risk control, financial control by visual image, a lightweight steering system which supersedes traditional budget management, the financial function, and certain aspects of human resource and information technology management which can only be handled at group level. In many banks, head office still interposes a screen between decisions required by the customers and action taken by the operational heads. A trimming of the center therefore remains an essential rite of passage in the expansion of a culture which favors development, innovation, and in-the-field problem-solving, in contrast to a mentality where priority goes to formal compliance with procedures. In the new perspective, the head office assumes the role of a holding group comprising a small team of executives who are both involved in strategic reflection and have a strong aptitude for action, based on a thorough knowledge of people and of the business, and the ability to work together. A corollary of this structure is the creation of subsidiaries endowed with real decision-making autonomy: this helps confer individual responsibility on location and rapid execution. In the holding group, the executives have the necessary time to define and manage the bank's future. By not being directly involved in day-to-day management, they are consequently in a position to undertake actions for which a long-term outlook is required. As long as the holding group exercises its power in a flexible and clear manner, in close relationship with the operational heads, it can ensure coherency.

Transformation is the key word which has characterized the banking environment for the past two decades and which will accelerate over the next two. It is taking place in front of our eyes at a rapid pace, both outside and within many banks. Only the final objective remains constant: each bank has to create for its customers and for itself maximum wealth. Lasting success in this area presupposes the reconciliation of two requirements, one based on ethics, the other on efficiency. In the words of Jean Fourastié: "The fundamental function of ethics is of the same nature as that of instinct, it is to ensure continuity of life." If tomorrow's bank is to be successful, it will have to rethink its principles of governance. Just as worship of the written word and of status hinders action, so can the values of risk assumption, transparency in information, rigor in management, and commitment to people and to the long-term view, induce real added value.

However, the qualitative dimension is not sufficient. It must be complemented by a relentless drive for professionalism which is especially necessary because the problems to be dealt with today are more complex than before. In our day and age, management of a great bank requires the implementation of a process which integrates the human, technical, and financial factors into a coherent order according to a process which continually modifies the firm's resources as market needs evolve. The future belongs to organizations that will be able to create this movement and to make it last.

◇

Notes

◆

NOTES TO CHAPTER 1

1 A systematic development of the strategic implications of technological progress can be found in A. Cotta, *Les choix économiques de la grande entreprise*, Paris, Dunod, 1969.
2 See Cotta, *Les choix économiques*, Paris, Dunod, 1969; *Théorie générale du capital, de la croissance et des fluctuations*, Paris, Dunod, 1962.
3 For an overview, see OECD, *Les télécommunications: perspectives d'évolution et stratégie des pouvoirs publics*, Paris, 1983.
4 For the economic aspects, mainly the consequences of such performances on the competition of telecommunications firms, two books are of interest: Meyer, Wilson et al., *The Economies of Competition in the Telecommunications Industry*, Oelgeschlager, Gunn & Hain, 1980; W. N. Sharkey, *The Theory of National Monopoly*, Cambridge University Press, 1982.
5 J. L. and M. J. Crombs, *Expert Systems: Concept and Examples*, NCC Publications, May 1984; A. Bonnet, *L'intelligence artificielle, promesses et réalités*, Inter-Editions, 1984.
6 I have drawn my inspiration largely from the article by Marie-Jeanne Maillot, "The prospect for expert systems and the issue they raise in banking," *Bank and Management*, September 1985.
7 J.-P. Aubert and R. Schomberg, *Pratiquez l'intelligence artificielle*, Eyrolles, March, 1985; W. Reitman, *Artificial Intelligence Applications for Business*, Ablex, 1984; Agence de l'Informatique, *International Days: Expert Systems and their Applications*, Avignon, France.
8 Bank for International Settlements, *Recent Innovations in International Banking*, April 1986.
9 See James E. Fitzpatrick, "Technology in banking in the 1980s," *Journal of the Institute of Bankers in Ireland*, 83, April 1981, pp. 74–85.

10 D. Thomson, "Credit cards: breaking down the frontiers," *Financial Times*, 23 May 1986.
11 Biometry is a set of personal prints determined at birth which remain constant, except in the case of major surgical intervention.
12 An allusive but enlightening article has been written by R. von Weizsäcker: "Free entry into telecommunications?" *Information Economics and Policy*, 1–3, 1984, pp. 197–216.
13 Donald R. Hodgman, *Commercial Bank Loan and Investment Policy*, Champaign, Ill., Bureau of Economic and Business Research, University of Illinois, 1963. For a theoretical reading, see Merton Miller and Daniel Orr, "A model of the demand for money by firms," *Quarterly Journal of Economics*, 80, August 1966, p. 413.
14 These figures are taken from internal studies carried out at the Midland Bank plc.
15 See the brief synthesis by G. Hewitt, "Technology, a two-edged sword for the banks," *Financial Times*, 23 May 1986.
16 This typology is the one adopted by Salomon Brothers, notably in its study, *Technology in Banking: A Path to Competitive Advantage*.
17 See National Commission on Electronic Fund Transfers, *International Payments Symposium*, Washington, DC, NCEFT, 1977; David S. Walker, "An analysis of EFTS activity levels, costs, and structure in the United States," *Journal of Bank Research*, Winter 1981, pp. 200–5.
18 See American Bankers Association, *Critical Issues in Banks Cards*, seminar, Washington, DC, 1980; Bank for International Settlements, *Payment Systems in 11 Developed Countries*, Basel, 1980.
19 For greater detail, see Georges C. White, "Developments in United States payments system." *Journal of Bank Research*, 11, Winter 1981, pp. 200–5.
20 For a theoretical view, see William J. Baumol, "The transactions demand for money: an inventory theoretical approach," *Quarterly Journal of Economics*, 66, November 1952; Raija H. Bettauer, "Joint EFT investments and bank services corporations," *Banking Law Journal*, 98, May 1981, pp. 432–48.
21 For greater details on this, see the OECD study, *Les banques et les transferts électroniques de fonds*, from which I drew much of my inspiration.
22 For a particular study, see Center for Business Research, *Retail Electronic Banking and Point of Sale*, Manchester, Center for Business Research, 1981.

23 The line taken here, as well as most of the product developments described in these paragraphs, draw their inspiration from the above mentioned Salomon Brothers study, *Technology in Banking*.
24 See Robert Park, "Banking by television," *Bankers' Magazine* (UK), 224, December 1980, pp. 13–14; Sandford Rose, "The frightening implications of EFT," *American Bankers*, 145, 30 January 1980, pp. 1–4.

NOTES TO CHAPTER 2

1 George J. Sigler, "A theory of oligopoly," *Journal of Political Economy*, February 1964; see also R. Cameron et al., *Banking in the Early Stages of Industrialization*, New York, Oxford University Press, 1967.
2 H. Bouquin, *Analyse microéconomique de la firme bancaire. Contribution à la recherche de l'optimum de la banque*, thesis for the doctorat d'Etat de Sciences économiques, Paris IX, 1974; J. Bouvier, *Un siècle de banque française. Les contraintes de l'Etat et les incertitudes des marchés*, Paris, Hachette, 1972.
3 G. F. Dumont, *Efficience et dimension des banques*, Paris, LGCJ, 1975.
4 A. L. Burns, *The Decline of Competition, 1950, 1936*, ch. 1; E. A. G. Robinson, *The Structure of Competitive Industry*, 1935.
5 See G. Benston, "Economies of scale and marginal costs in banks operations," in K. J. Cohen and F. S. Hammer (eds), *Analytical Methods in Banking*, Homewood, Irwin, 1966, pp. 544–75; G. Benston, "Economies of scale of financial institutions," *Journal of Money, Credit and Banking*, May 1972, pp. 312–41.
6 A. D. H. Kaplan, *Small Business: Its Place and Problems*, 1948.
7 "Profiles of live men in the global game," *Financial Times*, 23 May 1986.
8 From the abundant bibliography available, I have chosen two particularly concise accounts: Barry Riley, "Global expansion needs new capital," *Financial Times*, 23 February 1986; Lester Chandler, "Monopolistic elements in commercial banking," *Journal of Political Economy*, 46, 1938.
9 For a greater understanding of the process described here, see M. Mayer, *The Money Bazaars*, Edition E. D. Dutton, 1984.
10 "International financing of development," in *Revue économique*, special issue, Paris, Fondation nationale des Sciences politiques.

11 Report by the trilateral Commission: Martin Feldstein, Hervé de Carmoy, and K. Narusawa, *Restoring Growth in the Debt-Laden Third World*, 1987.
12 Mikuni and Co., October 1987.
13 For greater detail on this aspect, see Japan Trade Advisory Group, "The continuing competitive threat in financial and related services," *British Overseas Trade Board*.
14 In the last issue by IBM, the Japanese were also in charge of the operation.
15 See table 6.9 on the structure of Japanese payments.
16 It is noteworthy that the system of insurance by capitalization remains the principal plank of this success on account of the possibilities which it has given institutional investors. The fifteen leading British institutional investors manage funds exeeding $200 bn.
17 P. de Weck, "Les banques en Suisse et leurs relations avec l'étranger," *Revue économique et Société*, December 1972, pp. 315–23; J. Denizet, "Evolution récente et future de la banque," *Revue d'Economie politique*, May–June 1970, pp. 448–74.
18 P. Brundsen, "Building a US branch network," *The Banker*, January 1974, pp. 37–47 and "Here come foreign banks again," *Business Week*, 26 June 1978, pp. 78–86.
19 S. de Brunhoff, *La politique monétaire*, Paris, PUF, 1973; A. Chaineau, "Mécanismes et politiques monétaires," *Economie des intermédiares financiers*, Paris, Economica, 1974.
20 S. W. Robinson, *Multinational Banking: A Study of Certain Legal and Financial Aspects of the Postwar Operations of the US Branch Banks in Western Europe*, Leiden, A. W. Sijthoff, 1972.
21 The following lines are based on the Group of Thirty study, *Japan's Role in the Emerging Global Securities Markets*.
22 Mikuni and Co., 1987.
23 H. G. Grubel, "A theory of multinational banking," *Banca nazionale del Lavoro Quarterly Review*, December 1977, pp. 349–52; P. Genet, "La banque dans un monde en voie d'intégration," report of the 27th session of the International Banking Summer School, Aulanko, May–June 1974, *Banque*, January 1975, pp. 27–34.
24 F. H. Klopstock, "Les tendances qui se font jour dans les opérations bancaires à l'échelle internationale," *Revue de la Société d'Etudes et d'Expansion*, September–October 1970, pp. 730–7; J. S. W. Coombs, "The growing strength of regional banks,"

The Banker, September 1977, pp. 103–5. The Norin Chukin Bank is an example.

25 OECD, *The Internationalization of Banking*, Paris, 1977; Ruffini, *Banques multinationales et système bancaire transnational*, Paris, PUF, IRFM (state doctoral dissertation).

26 The Banker Research Unit, *Who Owns What in World Banking 1977–1978*, London, 1978; P. A. Wellons, *Transnational Banks*, UN Report to the Center on Transnational Corporations, December 1976.

27 William Hall, "Greater attention to domestic business," *Financial Times* (survey), February 1986.

28 See A. Cotta, *Les cinque erreurs, L'émergence de nouveaux rentiers*, Paris, Orban, 1985.

29 See all the finance literature on the intertemporal balance and correlative models of optimalization. One of the more recent publications is Cox, Ingersoll, Ross, *A Rational Anticipation Intertemporal Asset Pricing Theory*.

30 I recommend a study that unfortunately only deals with the case in Canada: L. R. Fite, "Competition and corporation in the evolution of the Canadian payment system," *The World of Banking*, July–August 1982.

31 On the subsequent evolution of the exchange market in relationship with the strategic considerations developed here, see the first part of the study by the Group of Thirty, *The Foreign Exchange Market in the 1980s: The Views of Market Participants*, New York.

32 See with regard to this: R. W. Eisenmenger, Mundell, Weiss, "Pricing and the role of the federal reserve in an electronic funds transfer system," in *Federal Reserve Bank of Boston*, pp. 97–110.

NOTES TO CHAPTER 3

1 See speech by Anthony M. Salomon, President of the Federal Reserve Bank of New York, at the National Bankers Association on Wednesday 17 October 1984, entitled: "Banking deregulation: where do we go from here."

2 See: *Review of the Federal Reserve Bank of Saint-Louis*; Board of Government of the Federal Reserve System, *Annual Statistical Digest*, 1941–1970, 1970–9; Elijah Brewer et al., *The Depository*

Institutions Deregulation and Monetary Control Act of 1980, Federal Reserve Bank of Chicago, September–October; Thomas Cargill and Gillian Garcia, *Financial Deregulation and Monetary Control*, Washington DC, Hoover Institution, 1982: Eugène Fama, "What's different about banks?" *Journal of Monetary Economics*, January 1981, pp. 29–39; R. Alton Gilbert, "Effectiveness of state reserve requirements," and R. Alton Gilbert and Jean M. Lovati, "Bank reserve requirements in their enforcement: a comparison across states," *Review of the Federal Reserve Bank of Saint-Louis*, March 1978, pp. 22–32; L. Goldberg and John T. Rose, "The effect on non member banks of the imposition of member bank reserve requirements," *Journal of Finance*, December 1976, pp. 1457–69; Christopher James, "An analysis of intra-industry differences in the effect of regulation: the case of deposit rate ceilings," *Journal of Monetary Economics*, September 1983; Robert E. Knight, "Reserve requirements, Part 1: Comparative reserve requirements at member and non member banks," Federal Reserve Bank of Kansas City, *City Monthly Review*, April 1974, pp. 3–20; *Financial Institutions Deregulation and Monetary Control*, Commerce Clearing House Inc., 1980; G. J. C. Santoni, "The monetary control act, renove taxes and the stock prices of commercial banks," *Review of the Federal Reserve Bank of Saint-Louis*, June–July 1985, vol. 67, no. 6, pp. 12–20.

3 See *Bulletin de conjoncture Paribas* on American deregulation.

4 See A. Cotta, *Les cinque erreurs, L'émergence de nouveaux rentiers*, Paris, Orban, 1985.

5 Junk bonds are bonds issued by a company with the aim of buying back its capital. See the discussion of the Drexel Burnham Lambert case in chapter 6 below.

6 I include almost in their entirety, making them more explicit, the three points referred to in *Bulletin de conjoncture Paribas*, p. 152, para. 2.

7 Cooke Report, 1987.

8 On the nature of the British banking system, see Sir John Clapham, *The Bank of England*, Cambridge University Press, 1944; Committee of London Clearing Bankers, *The London Clearing Banks*, London, Longman, 1978.

9 For details of the British banking system, see Report of the Treasury Committee on Bank Amalgamations (Colwyn Report), Cd 9052, London, HMSO, 1918; Report of the Committee on

Finance and Industry (Macmillan Report), Cmd 3897, HMSO, 1931; also Minutes of Evidence.

10 See M. Mayer, *The Money Bazaars*, Edition E. D. Dutton, 1984.

11 See A. Cotta, *Les choix économiques de la grande entreprise*, Paris, Dunod, 1969; Report of the Committee on Company Law Amendment (Cohen report), London, HMSO, 1945; Report of the Committee on the Working of the Monetary System (Radcliffe Report), London, HMSO, 1959; also Memoranda and Minutes of Evidence: Minutes of Evidence taken before Company Law Committee (Jenkins Committee), 16 December 1960, London, HMSO, 1961; Monopolies Commission, Barclays Bank Ltd, Lloyds Bank Ltd and Martins Bank Ltd, London, HMSO, 1978; Committee to Review the Functioning of Financial Institutions (Wilson Committee), Second Stage Evidence, vol. 4, London, HMSO, 1979.

12 Alton R. Gilbert, C. Stone Courtenay, and Michael E. Treblin, "The new bank capital adequacy standards," *Review of the Federal Reserve Bank of Saint-Louis*, May 1985, vol. 67, no. 5; G. A. Hanneck and J. J. Mingo, *External Capital Financing Requirements of Commercial Banks, 1977–1981,* New York, Federal Reserve Board, 1978; Y. E. Orgler and B. Wolkowitz, *Bank Capital*, New York, Van Nostrand Reinhold, 1978; B. K. Short, Capital requirements for commercial banks, IMF Staff Paper, September 1978; G. J. Vojta, "Bank capital adequacy," *Citybank* 1973; "A dynamic view of capital adequacy," *Journal of Commercial Bank Lending*, December 1974. See also along the same lines, J. Revell, *Solvency and Regulation of Banks*, Cardiff, University of Wales Press, 1975; C. R. Wittlesey and J. S. G. Wilson (eds), *Essays in Money and Banking*, Oxford, Clarendon Press, 1968, esp. chs 9 and 10 on banking ratios by J. E. Wadsworth; L. S. Presswell, "That liquidity ratio," *Journal of the Institute of Bankers*, 1959; "The capital and liquidity adequacy of banks," *Bank of England Quarterly Bulletin*, September 1975.

13 *Costs and Margins in Banking: An International Survey*, Paris, OECD, 1980.

14 See the abundant literature devoted to this, in particular: "Advertisement: raising over $1 billion of capital for commercial banks in 1984 through the sale of real estate," *Wall Street Journal*, 30 January 1985; "Agriculture: FDIC study says farm bank failures largely due to mismanagement," *Daily Report for Execu-*

tives, DER 56, Bureau of National Affairs, 22 March 1985, p. L–5; "Bank crisis tied to drop in confidence," *New York Journal of Commerce*, 8 April 1985; "Banking confidence may emerge as a potent political issue," *Wall Street Journal*, 8 April 1985; Laurent Belsie, "Troubled times for farmers will weed out the rural banks," *Christian Science Monitor*, 10 April 1985; William E. Blundell, "As basic institutions like phones and banks change, public chafes," *Wall Street Journal*, 5 February 1985; John F. Childs, Letter to the Editor, *American Banker*, 18 January 1985; Department of the Treasury, "Deposit insurance study forwarded to CCEA," *Treasury News*, 15 January 1985; Federal Deposit Insurance Corporation, "Deposit insurance in a changing environment," in *A Report to Congress on Federal Deposit Insurance*, appendix B, 15 April 1983; "More bank failures to come," *The Economist*, 23 March 1985; Office of the Comptroller of the Currency, *Final Regulatory Impact Analysis*, 1985; Kenneth B. Noble, "New capital suggested to make banks safer," *New York Times*, 11 January 1985; G. David Wallace and Riemer Blanca, "More capital for banks: the cure may be worse than the disease," *Business Week*, 28 January 1985.

15 G. Rae, *The Country Banker*, letter XXXV.

NOTES TO CHAPTER 4

1 See The United States Department of Labor, 1984, Bureau of Labor Statistics.

2 On this evolution in the United States, see Benjamin M. Friedman, "Postwar changes in the American financial markets," in Martin Feldstein (ed.), *The American Economy in Transition*, Washington DC, National Bureau of Economic Research, 1980, p. 4.

3 Bank Administration Institute, *Checking Account Usage in the United States*, 1979.

4 *Changes in US Bank Offices*, New York, Federal Deposit Insurance Corporation, 1984.

5 United States Department of Labor, Bureau of Labor Statistics, *Employment and Earnings*, Washington DC, 1984.

6 See OECD study.

7 Douglas McGregor, *Hommes et organisations. La Profession de manager*, Charles Riley Consultant. I would like to thank Charles

Riley for his contribution in this area in the course of ten years of collaboration.

8 On the different types of conflicts, see the interesting article by Hans J. Thamhain and David L. Wilemon, "Leadership, conflict and program management effectiveness," in *Sloan Management Review*, Fall 1977.

9 March and Simon, *Les organisations*, Paris, Dunod, p. 111.

10 David L. Wilemon and Hans J. Thamhain, "Conflict management in project life cycles," *Sloan Management Review*, Spring 1975, p. 31.

11 Hill, "Managing conflict in project teams," *Sloan Management Review*, Winter 1977, p. 46.

12 Clagett Smith, *A Comparative Analysis of some Conditions and Consequences of Intraorganizational Conflict*.

NOTES TO CHAPTER 5

1 *New York Times*, 4 August 1989.

2 Fama, Blume, "Filter rules and stock trading," *Journal of Business*, 39 January 1966; Granger, Morgenstern, "Spectral analysis of New York stock market prices," *Kylos*, 16, 1963; Levasseur, "Comment varient les cours sur le marché de Paris," *Cahier de recherche du CESA*, 6, 1973.

NOTES TO CHAPTER 6

1 Data source: IDD Information Services.

2 Federal Reserve Bank of New York, Recent Trends in Commercial Bank Profitability, a Staff Study, New York, 1986.

3 Twenty-three of the last fifty of the top 200 American banks have a rate of return on total assets of over 1 percent, while among the first twenty-three only Morgan reaches this level of profitability (*Business Week*, 1986).

4 Mikuni and Co., September 1987.

5 Georges Bataille, *La part maudite*, Paris, Gallimard, vol. 7; Alexandre Kojève, *Introduction à la lecture de Hegel*, Paris, Gallimard.

Index

Page numbers in italics refer to figures and tables